THE CHOICE OF THE FAMILY

THE
CHOICE
OF THE
FAMILY

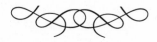

A Call to Wholeness, Abundant Life,
and Enduring Happiness

Bishop Jean Laffitte

Foreword by Carl Anderson
Preface by Archbishop Charles J. Chaput
Interviews with Pierre and Véronique Sanchez
Translated by Rev. Gregory Gresko

IMAGE
NEW YORK

Published in the United States by Image, an imprint of the
Crown Publishing Group, a division of Penguin Random House LLC, New York.

www.crownpublishing.com

IMAGE is a registered trademark and the "I" colophon is a
trademark of Penguin Random House LLC.

Originally published in French in Canada as *Le Choix de la Famille* by Jean Laffitte,
published by L'échelle de Jacob in VISAGE. Copyright © 2011 by L'échelle de Jacob.

"Preface" by Archbishop Charles Chaput. Used by permission of the author.

Library of Congress cataloging-in-publication data
is available upon request

ISBN 978-0-553-44753-8
eISBN 978-0-553-44754-5

Printed in the United States of America

Book design by Jennifer Daddio / Bookmark Design & Media Inc.
Jacket design: Jessie Sayward Bright
Jacket illustration: Tilia Foemina, Lindenbaum, or Lime Tree, illustration from
De hisotria stirpium (woodcut), Fuchs, Leonhard (1502–66) / Private Collection /
The Stapleton Collection / Bridgeman Images

1   3   5   7   9   10   8   6   4   2

First Edition

To Robert and Jeanne

CONTENTS

ACKNOWLEDGMENTS

I owe a special debt of gratitude to Carl Anderson, Supreme Knight of the Knights of Columbus, and to all of the Knights of Columbus for their substantial support and collaboration in this work.

I deeply appreciate the invaluable expertise of Dr. Michelle Borras in editing the English translation, and for her generous availability in preparing the final text.

It is our mutual prayer that all families come to understand more profoundly God's design for human love through the labors of this project.

THE CHOICE OF THE FAMILY

Foreword

THE CHOICE OF THE FAMILY

Carl Anderson[1]

The Christian life we are called to live within the family is not something just to be studied. It is something to be lived. And it is something to be lived with joy.

Every family—believing and nonbelieving alike—is a unique expression of the universal experience of family life. Each family exists within a living ecology—a unique environment shaped by the dynamism of its members, who present a variety of age, health, maturity, responsibility, ability, personality, and aspiration. No institution in society can shape and, in so many ways, determine a person's life to the same extent as the man and woman who give one life, and the family with which one shares one's formative years.

At the same time, the family is also a school of transcendence. By its very existence, the family points each of its members toward the future in a context of hope. The journey of the family is in this way a journey toward transcendence. In opening the person to this horizon of transcendence, the family becomes

---

1 Supreme Knight, Knights of Columbus

the most universal way in which a person is introduced not only to the concept of God, but to the experience of Him. The family is a sign of God's love as well as a manifestation of Him *as* love. While the love of spouses, parents, children, and siblings is often the benchmark of human love itself, the very structure of the family points us to a greater love as its own model. The family opens up to each of its members a vocation to serve life that is inherently and intimately collaborative with the God who is the author of life.

The Christian family presents the believer with this vocation, which finds its true meaning by cooperating with the vocations of the other members of the family, thus creating a unique union of vocations. Thus we may consider the Christian family as a great dialogue among persons who are at the same time engaged in a dialogue with God.

Pope Francis expressed this reality beautifully:

> *The image of God is the married couple: the man and the woman; not only the man, not only the woman, but both of them together. This is the image of God: love, God's covenant with us, is represented in that covenant between man and woman. And this is very beautiful! We are created in order to love, as a reflection of God and his love. And in the marital union man and woman fulfill this vocation through their mutual reciprocity and their full and definitive communion of life.*[2]

The Catholic Church's vision of family stems not merely from a knowledge of families gained through an experience of family life or through the experience of serving families, but from a

---

2 Pope Francis, General Audience, April 2, 2014.

knowledge of the God who is love and who gave the human race the institution of the family—an institution in which He makes Himself present. Therefore, the Christian sees the family in its essence as an institution that calls each of its members to a vocation shaped by love.

In every family, just as in every marriage, there are times when each person becomes keenly aware that his or her vocation to love demands a radical decisiveness. Every family in its journey will make decisions that call its members closer to a life in Christ and to authentic happiness—or farther away. At times, one's vocation of family entails a conscious decision, an orienting of one's life in a new direction out of love and in the embrace of the other. At other times, this vocation entails embracing a reality that is the result of a decision not our own, as when one becomes a grandparent or when a new sibling is born. But in each instance, our vocation requires the decisiveness of a love that is open and generous.

The richness of family life makes the family an irresistible subject of study. But it is a subject that is not capable of being understood in an abstract way or for abstract reasons. It is not possible to truly know the family unless we know the active, concrete experience of family life, and this requires us to admit that there is no better school of the family than the family itself.

Catholics, especially those whose daily life and vocation center around the family, have received a great gift: the numerous Church leaders in recent years who have been so grounded in their own family experiences that they have brought profound theological insight and devotion to their pastoral approach to the family.

In the theological approach of Pope Benedict XVI we see the fundamental importance of personal communion to our encounter with truth—an encounter which is opened to us first within the family:

*Truth is not an imposition. Nor is it simply a set of rules. It is a
discovery of the One who never fails us; the One whom we can
always trust. In seeking truth we come to live by belief because
ultimately truth is a person: Jesus Christ. That is why authentic
freedom is not an opting out. It is an opting in; nothing less than
letting go of self and allowing oneself to be drawn into Christ's
very being for others.*[3]

And with Pope Francis it is evident that the vocation of
Christian spouses is a clear path to understanding their call to
discipleship *through the family.*

*Christian matrimony is a lifelong covenant of love between
one man and one woman; it entails real sacrifices in order
to turn away from illusory notions of sexual freedom and in
order to foster conjugal fidelity. Your programs of preparation for the sacrament of matrimony, enriched by Pope John
Paul's teaching on marriage and the family, are proving to
be promising and indeed indispensable means of communicating the liberating truth about Christian marriage and are
inspiring young people with new hope for themselves and for
their future as husbands and wives, fathers and mothers.*[4]

Of course, both Pope Benedict and Pope Francis have
brought forward their pastoral ministry within the context of
the family ministry of St. John Paul II. No pope in history devoted as much time and attention to the pastoral care of the

---

3 Pope Benedict XVI, Meeting with Young People, Yonkers, New York, April 19, 2008.

4 Pope Francis, Address for the Ad Limina Visit of bishops from South Africa,
April 25, 2014.

Christian family as did St. John Paul II—whom Pope Francis described, at his canonization, as the pope of the family.

With the publication of *The Choice of the Family*, Bishop Jean Laffitte has added to this richness in the Church's understanding of the Christian family as both a community that evangelizes, and the subject of evangelization.

Bishop Laffitte and I had the great privilege of coming to know St. John Paul II in a personal way because of our work together at the Pontifical John Paul II Institute for Studies on Marriage and Family. We were colleagues at the Institute: both as faculty members and as vice presidents. In the course of this collaboration it became evident that it was not merely the depth of John Paul's understanding—of the nature of the human person and personal communion in marriage and the family—that inspired the Institute's work. It was also the *way* in which this understanding was achieved and transmitted. An adequate understanding of marriage and family could never be achieved simply at an abstract or juridical level—it is always necessary to ground this understanding of family life in concrete experience. This grounding in the "bright spots and shadows" of the family brought to John Paul a realism and affection for family life, as well as the firm conviction of the fundamental goodness and importance of families.

St. John Paul II often said that the family is the primary way of the Church. If his ministerial devotion to families had a motto, it would perhaps be this: "Family, become what you are!"[5] It captures the inherent identity existing in a family by virtue of its being a family, and the continual transformation of a family toward living out its mission in a holy, authentic, and joy-filled way.

---

5 Pope John Paul II, *Familiaris Consortio*, §17.

I think readers who are familiar with these popes will similarly be very warmed by Bishop Laffitte's own insights, which take the reader through various experiences, stages, and choices of love in the vocations of familial communion. The depth of his insight is matched by the clarity with which he expresses it, and shows to the reader a man whose affection for the family has led him to devote much of his own life to inspiring others to experience the full richness of the vocation to marriage and family life. *The Choice of the Family* exemplifies, in a very concrete way, God's instruction to Moses to "choose life, that you and your descendants may live" (Deut. 30:19).

Today there is a great focus on parenting—on the reality of being a parent and "having" a child. But Bishop Laffitte begins at our true beginning, with the first and only universal experience of family: that of being a child. His book wisely begins with this experience, and the depth of awareness both of the individuality of Bishop Laffitte's personal family and of the universal experience of family. *The Choice of the Family* invites the reader to understand in a more profound way the experience of his or her own family, and in so doing to acquire a new, joyful embrace of family life.

The Choice of the Family is a testament to the joy of the Christian family fully alive. Bishop Laffitte's own joy of being Christian—the joy of a deep, vibrant, expansive friendship with Christ, whose very life as God is one of a communion of persons—permeates this book with vitality, and provides an appreciation for the Catholic vision of the family that is at once a practical and a sublime guide for every Catholic family seeking to become who they are.

Preface

When the Church speaks of "vocation," she means the "calling out" of each human person to accomplish a task preordained by God in the coredemption of the world. Every human being has a vocation. God created each individual soul with a specific purpose in mind. Thus, the greatest joy for a Christian is pursuing the purpose for which God created him or her.

To put it another way, the idea of vocation implies a design to our lives. It also implies a Designer, since Somebody greater than ourselves must create us for the task we're meant to accomplish.

For Christians, marriage is a vocation. And by "marriage," we mean much more than a legal contract. We mean a permanent, sacramental covenant between one man and one woman; two persons becoming one flesh. That covenant is ordered toward procreation, and toward mutual love and holiness. And within it, God plays a very active role as a third partner.

This understanding of marriage is increasingly uncomfortable for the modern mind. Permanence seems implausible. Children are often avoided as liabilities. And the very idea of holiness can seem like a pious delusion. In contrast, Christians—at least those Christians who seek seriously to live their faith—believe in a loving, personal, approachable Creator who knows each of us by name, and who seeks our eternal happiness. For the

Christian, all created things have meaning. They're part of a symphony giving glory to the Lord of life.

The alternatives to a healthy marriage culture are sobering. Children in single-parent families are far more likely to be poor, and they stay poor longer. They're more likely to have emotional and behavioral problems. They're more likely to fail in the classroom and to drop out of school completely, to become pregnant as teenagers, to abuse drugs and get into trouble with the law.

They're also at much higher risk for physical and sexual abuse. Children from disrupted families have a harder time achieving intimacy in their relationships, forming stable marriages, and holding steady employment. In other words, contrary to the European and North American mythology of the past fifty years, divorce is a disaster for children.

The family—by its very structure—is a rejection of fear and an expression of hope. Its natural fertility brings the future into human flesh. It is the engine of life. It has real power. It's the doorway by which God enters into humanity. This is why the modern state so often seeks to control or redefine the family—to break it down, even when the practical results of that breakdown are so obviously damaging. The family is a competing, sovereign source of meaning that precedes and stands apart from the state. It demands unselfishness. It teaches community. It inculcates higher values, which claim the moral authority to order our actions and our material appetites.

Today, for this reason, the vocation of marriage is a call to both loving resistance and missionary zeal: resistance to the culture of materialism and infertility, and zeal to spread the truth about the nature of the human person, which is fully revealed only in Jesus Christ.

Christian marriage is not a passive state. Love is active. It creates new life. It thereby renews humanity and the face of the entire earth. It's an echo, in human flesh, of the love within the Trinity itself. Every moment of every day, a mother and father are teaching, guiding, and sanctifying each other and their children, while witnessing about their love to the world beyond the borders of their home. They can't do otherwise. The structure of marriage, if lived fruitfully and faithfully, naturally takes them down this road.

The marital covenant provides the kind of reassurance to both spouses that enables them to surrender themselves fully to each other. In doing that, they become the most basic living cell of society. Marriage is the foundation and guarantee of the family, and the family is the foundation and guarantee of society.

Nothing else will serve as a grounding for the common good—not government, not technology, not shared economic interests. This is why St. John Paul II wrote, in his 1994 *Letter to Families*, "No human society can run the risk of permissiveness on fundamental issues regarding the nature of marriage and the family. Such moral permissiveness [can only] damage the authentic requirements of peace and communion among people."

It's within the intimate, personal community of the family that a child, in observing his or her parents, first learns those basic values—such as loyalty, honesty, and selfless concern for others—which build up the character of the wider society. Truth is always most persuasive *not* when we read about it in a book or hear about it in a classroom, but when we see it, firsthand, incarnated in the actions of our parents.

The family safeguards our fundamental sense of community,

because within it the child grows up in a web of intimately connected rights and responsibilities to other people. But it also protects our unique, individual identity, because it shields the child with a mantle of privacy and personal devotion. And again, *that's* where the enduring power of marriage and family lies. We most easily understand and believe in love when we—ourselves—are the fruit of our parents' tenderness and fidelity. Love lived well is the unanswerable argument for God—and also for the worthiness of the human heart.

The nature of the human condition is that we are always either growing or dying. We must choose life or death. There is no middle ground. In Deuteronomy, God says to his people, "I have set before you life and death, the blessing and the curse. Choose life then, that you and your descendants may live" (30:19).

Every marriage that makes an act of trust in God and remains open to children is a powerful choice for life. And to the glory of the Church—despite all the hostility of the modern world—she keeps those words of the Creator alive in humanity's heart and conscience.

It's my privilege to have as a friend one of the finest sons of the Church today in preaching and defending the dignity of the family. In his ministry as a priest, bishop, and secretary of the Pontifical Council for the Family, Jean Laffitte's contribution to the Christian understanding of marriage and family in the modern world has been invaluable. The interviews with Bishop Laffitte that make up the book you're about to read reveal a man of compassion, intelligence, and deep love for the vocation of married couples and families.

In Bishop Laffitte's own words, "Love is always good news, and it is good news that is always accessible"—whether a person is rich, poor, famous, or unknown. The vocation of marriage, the "choice of the family," is not the only Christian path to meaning and joy; but it's the invitation most men and women will hear from the loving God who made them. It's a call to wholeness, to abundant life, to enduring happiness. And very few people grasp that fact more deeply or speak of it more articulately than the man you will encounter in these pages.

—*Charles J. Chaput, O.F.M. Cap. Archbishop of Philadelphia*

Under the abstract words of paternity . . . I have come to believe that, far from being endowed with an absolute existence of my own, I am, without having wished or suspected it, I incarnate the reply to the reciprocal appeal which two beings flung to each other in the unknown and which, without suspecting it, they flung beyond themselves to an incomprehensible power whose only expression is the bestowal of life. I am this reply, unformed at first, but who, as I become articulate, will know myself to be a reply and a judgment. Yes, I am irresistibly led to make the discovery that by being what I am, I myself am a judgment upon those who have called me into being; and thereby infinite new relationships will be established between them and me.

GABRIEL MARCEL, HOMO VIATOR

ONE

Your Journey

For the Son of God, Jesus Christ, whom we preached among you . . . was not Yes and No; but in Him it is always Yes. For all the promises of God find their Yes in Him. That is why we utter the Amen through Him, to the glory of God.

(2 COR. 1:18–20)

Pierre and Véronique Sanchez: *Bishop, before tackling a few aspects concerning marriage and the family, could you tell us who you are, and what is your expertise? We asked to do this book with you because after encountering you, we perceived that you were not simply an official of the Church, either within the framework of your formation or within your work, or within your faith . . . Like everyone else, you come from a family, and from a large family? Could you tell us about it?*

Bishop Jean Laffitte: I indeed belong to a large family. My father was a surgeon and my parents, who both are now deceased, certainly inculcated into each one of us a love for life and for family values. I say this simply because I know that there was from them this attitude of welcoming all the children that the Lord wanted to entrust to them. They had twelve children, and I am the twelfth! We are six girls and six boys. I have many nephews and nieces, great nephews and great nieces. To give you an idea, my parents today have one hundred descendants. It happens still, in spite of everyone's occupations, that on the occasion of a family reunion, we come together in very great number.

We lived in a city of the Pyrénées, Oloron-Sainte-Marie. The professional activity of my father was very absorbing. He worked in two clinics that were thirty-two kilometers from each other, Oloron in Béarn and Mauléon in the Basque country. There is a certain medical tradition in our family as my maternal grandfather also was a surgeon, and my uncles of that side were specialist physicians. After the fact, it is easy to reread the past, but I tell myself that it was within this context that I acquired an interest in family values. When I was young, I thought they were obvious, and I didn't reflect on them. It took a strong Christian commitment to realize how much the family was at the heart of social life and of Christian life. As children, we had before us the example in my parents of a great love for life; perhaps from there has come this interest that we share concerning all of the questions that touch upon human life.

In addition to these family values and those that touch upon human life—and it is in fact an essential point—my parents gave us a profoundly Christian education. They were both practicing Catholics. Each time they were able, they would go to Mass even during the week. It's an unbelievable thing when one thinks of my father's professional demands and the activity demanded of my mother for the smooth running of such a large household. To find the strength to go to Mass at seven a.m., in the great cathedral of Oloron, was at times heroic, especially when my parents had been disturbed during the night by emergencies. There is something there, that as a child one does not realize very well at the time, but as an adult one tells himself that he had before him an example of fidelity, of uprightness: That which our parents taught us, they lived. Of course, a large family has its traditions, its rituals, its ordeals, and its difficulties. Very concretely, a fundamental experience was lived, composed of several elements: the love of our parents and, at the same time, the relationships between brothers and sisters.

Christian education is carried out first by example. We never once saw our parents compromise their love for Christ and the Church. We were immersed in a climate of Christian sensibility and of familiarity with the life of the Church. The great family feasts were celebrated on the occasion of religious events: baptisms, first communions, marriages. It was a classic education of the 1950s and 1960s, with the seriousness that one gives to things of faith, along with that which is somewhat particular to the southwest of France, a point of view that sometimes can be a bit pessimistic. My parents were fundamental optimists, though: They trusted in Divine Providence. They were attentive to transmitting values within the cultural context that existed in France during those years. Concerning family roots, let's say that my father was originally from Béarn, from a small village in the Pyrénées-Atlantiques area near Orthez, Sallespisse. Over the course of many generations, his family had become landowners. He worked a lot, even receiving first place in the prestigious competition for medical students called *Internat* (Bordeaux) before the war, before becoming little by little a medical authority in the southwest of France. He also had been president of the students of France. On my mother's side are roots from the Périgord region, from Charentes, and also from Lorraine on my maternal grandmother's side.

What are the qualities that your education developed and that now have come to be most useful to you in your adult life and work, in your ministry?

J.L. At home, I saw and learned the concerns of humble people. I never saw any smugness or arrogance in them. The Béarnaise society of this average town was predominantly rural. The patients whom my father treated were above all farmers but factory workers as well, as the town also contained several factories and manufacturers. I always saw in my parents an extreme respect for simple people. In a small town during the 1950s, the family of a surgeon necessarily was a family of notable people, but that did not express itself among us through a worldly life.

The second thing that I saw and learned was to take seriously questions concerning God. Each person can have difficulties in faith and in religious practice, and all of the paths are not smooth. But there was no flippancy in this matter: We could not consider religion as a superficial issue.

Another virtue that we could observe in my parents was a very strict sense of honesty. If I were to say in one word what personally strikes me even today, it would be their uprightness. Our parents were upright and oriented toward life. They could make mistakes at times, but there was no guile in them.

How did your parents share their educative responsibilities? Do you have concrete examples concerning this question?

J.L. The family model was simple: There were at the same time the great, strong personality of our father and the daily, attentive presence of our mother. Thus, there was a kind of complementarity between them, as well as a profound unity:

I never saw one take issue with the decision of the other. For us children, there was a coherence in what was transmitted. I would not say that every day was easy. *Obedience* was not an empty word and authority was not up for discussion. It must be said that it was a different cultural context. Nevertheless, there was a core consistency, borne by the fact that the authority of the two parents was common to them, even if it expressed itself differently for the father and for the mother.

What qualities of your mother stand out the most to you?

For all mothers, and in particular in large families, there is a daily service that begins early in the morning and ends late at night. You easily can imagine twelve children close in age. In the 1950s and 1960s, all of the services at the disposal of today's mothers were not available. I would say that our mother had an extreme sense of service, loving and personal. What was apparent in her was a fundamental benevolence, an active kindness, to which could be added great discretion in the respect of each child and his interior life. She saw each of her children as single and unique. She was a great woman of faith and goodness.

Could you speak to us about your relationships with your brothers and sisters?

J.L. The fact that we were so united helped generate a strong solidarity. You benefited from all the experience of others who have opened the doors before you. For the child that you are, each one of your brothers and sisters is a kind of touchstone within a realm. As we were very close to each other, I had the opportunity of experiencing personal and profound relationships with each of my brothers and sisters. I must say that there is a profound and lively joy whenever I see any of my eleven brothers or sisters. This joy is all the greater as their various families are added to ours, with the new generations. It is a gift from God that renews each one of us. It is a treasure for which I bless the Lord. We get together quite often.

Do you remember having suffered from anything in particular during your childhood or your youth that proved to be determining in your growing up as a young man? What helped you to overcome this suffering? Was the course direct, straight?

J.L. As regards myself, as a child and adolescent, I was forced to face the crisis that affected the Church during the 1960s. I suffered from it to the extent that something did not have the time to articulate itself well. The religious experience of my childhood had been beautiful and strong. I was a choirboy during the long years before the Second Vatican Council. After my adolescent years, I distanced myself little by little from the regular practice of my faith. So, much later, I had to adopt as my own the faith that I had received. After the fact, I realize well how life without daily contact with God—whether it be in prayer or in sacramental life—can generate problems or suffering. When you grow up, distancing yourself from faith creates uncertainty in your personal plan. It is a search that can be sorrowful at times.

Despite that, do you have the feeling that you always have lived in a logic of continuity?

J.L. Yes, after the fact; but at the time, it might be lived as a succession of broken lines.

Are there any events or meetings from your childhood and youth that have played a decisive role in encouraging you along the path that is now yours today?

J.L. Yes: to begin with, everything I received during childhood. Certain priests and also profoundly Christian friends played a role. Then, an important spiritual influence is connected to a particular place for me, the sanctuary of Our Lady of Bétharram, near Lourdes: I was a boarding student there, and I felt close to the spiritual figure of Saint Michel Garicoïts. There also is Lourdes, of course, as well as another Marian sanctuary to which I was very devoted, Our Lady of Sarrance, in the Aspe Valley. Much later, during my adult life, two events were crucial: meeting with John Paul II, who would be for me a continual source of inspiration, and the Emmanuel Community, the path I walked for nearly thirty years.

But before these essential experiences, I must say that I am the godson of a man of the cloth: My godfather was the bishop of Aire and Dax, Monsignor Clément Matthieu, who had a profound impact on his diocese and died in 1963. I remember a few meetings with him, intimidating for the child that I was, with this important person. Monsignor Matthieu had been a disciple of Cardinal Mercier at Louvain before the war. He was an excellent professor in dogmatics. It is possible to find there a kind of spiritual sonship. And why this bishop? He had simply blessed the marriage of my parents, with whom he was connected in friendship. He had said to them one day, "I will be the godfather of the twelfth." And as my parents had twelve children, my parents took his word for it!

Within the family context, how was your vocation born? How was it welcomed by your parents and by your brothers and sisters?

How did your family help you along your journey toward the priesthood?

J.L. My vocation made itself known during my adult years, within the context that I have pointed out to you of a non-practicing faith. I have remained very sensitive today to persons whom I perceive believe in God without having the consistency of honoring their religious faith by faithful practice. It is something that has touched me deeply and also has inspired much pastoral contact within my priestly and episcopal ministry, especially through my teaching. It was at the age of thirty-two that I underwent a very strong conversion, in the midst of a trip to Rome, during Holy Week. It was a very lively and personal encounter with the resurrected Christ during the course of the Easter Vigil presided over by the future Blessed John Paul II. This faith that had been dormant for many long years became a living faith, centered on the event of meeting with the person of Christ. Everything changed from that moment. I was working at the time in banking, in Frankfurt, Germany. The desire to become a priest came upon me very quickly, and the bishop of Autun sent me to the French Seminary in Rome. My family very much welcomed this vocation. It is impossible for me to say at which point my family assisted me the most along my way, as much by prayer as by fraternal affection. It was a very great joy as well for my mother. My father already was deceased.

And the years that preceded this change in your life?

I had completed my secular studies in political science at Toulouse before spending two years cooperating on a project in Cameroon, teaching French, history, and geography. These years gave me an initial international openness and at the

same time an awareness that the world is infinitely larger than
what you perceive when you are living as a student in a university town. I then set about learning languages by way of long
studies abroad in Germany, then in Italy, Scotland, and finally
in Spain. In reality, it was a deciding factor in my life. At the
time, it facilitated my entry into active professional life; but
today, this choice has proven to be providential to the extent
that I am led in my present ministry to speak in these different
languages.

Priestly vocation or religious?

J.L. Truly priestly. The desire to celebrate the Holy Eucharist
and to give the forgiveness of Christ very clearly has accompanied that of transmitting the Word of God and of bearing witness. It is within the Emmanuel Community that I discovered
the importance of the Holy Spirit in the Christian life as well
as the power of the testimony of fraternal charity. Also involved
was the discovery of Paray-le-Monial and the message of the
Heart of Christ to Saint Margaret Mary. At the beginning of
the following university school year, I entered the seminary. So
I completed my philosophical and theological studies, at first at
the Gregorian University, and then at the John Paul II Institute
for the licentiate and doctorate in moral theology.

*Were you among the "first generation" formed at the John Paul II
Institute?*

J.L. In a certain sense, yes, at least as far as French students
are concerned. I had the opportunity, as did many others, to
benefit from the unforgettable teachings of Professors Carlo Caffarra and Angelo Scola, the two first presidents of the Institute,

who gave to this institution its current form; and, in addition, Stanislaw Grygiel was my thesis director. A close friend and disciple of Karol Wojtyła, he accompanied my research that was consecrated to a theological anthropology of pardon.[6]

And then you became a professor at the John Paul II Institute?

J.L. I knew many other professors as a student at the Institute, such as for example the Biblicist Ignace de la Potterie, the patrologist Henri Crouzel, the theologians Inos Biffi and Ramón García de Haro, the philosopher Josef Seifert, and so many others. It is impossible to mention all of them. Having become a professor myself, it was as a simple confrère and above all as a friend, that I came to know the next generation of teachers, Livio Melina (the current president), Marc Ouellet, Mario Binasco, Sergio Belardinelli, Claudio Giuliodori, Gilfredo Marengo, Giovanni Reale, Bruno Ognibeni, Giovanni Salmeri, José Noriega, Jaroslav Merecki, José Granados, and still many others, in particular in the other branches of the Institute. I think as well of Carl Anderson and David Schindler in Washington, Anthony Fisher and Tracey Rowland in Melbourne, Joao Carlos Petrini in Salvador de Bahia, Juan José Perez Soba in Madrid, and Juan Antonio Reig Pla in Valencia. Today, there are new generations of teachers, many of whom themselves were formed at the Institute. Numerous former students have risen today to levels of great responsibility in the Church.

Beyond the personal mark that a particular teaching can leave on students, the Institute has represented and still represents, for

---

6 Cf. Jean Laffitte, *Le Pardon Transfiguré*. Paris: Éditions de l'Emmanuel–Desclée, 1995.

each one of us—student or professor—a unique intellectual and human experience. This is due without a doubt to the richness of inspiration of its founder, whom we honor today as Blessed John Paul II. A true transmission of content transpires in moral theology, in philosophical and theological anthropology, in sacramental theology, and also in the humanities. Personally, I continue to ensure teaching in conjugal spirituality. The John Paul II Institute has just celebrated its thirtieth anniversary.

Before teaching, did you exercise other ministries?

J.L. I was ordained a priest in 1989 in Autun. In 1990, the bishop of Autun, Monsignor Raymond Séguy, named me as superior of the chaplains of Paray-le-Monial and entrusted to me two rural parishes near Charolles. He also asked me to do a doctoral thesis. That moment consequently was the beginning of a very dense ministry that involved animating the pilgrimages at Paray-le-Monial. After the defense of my thesis, I successively became the assistant of Professor Caffarra, then one year later of Professor Scola. In 2003, John Paul II named me as consultor at the Congregation for the Doctrine of the Faith, and in 2005 as undersecretary of the Pontifical Council for the Family. Benedict XVI then named me to the Pontifical Academy for Life, where I worked as well with Monsignor Elio Sgreccia, the greatest specialist in bioethics in the Catholic Church. The Pontifical Academy for Life, created by John Paul II, reunites scientists, philosophers, and theologians around questions pertaining to the ethics of life.

Finally, on October 22, 2009, Benedict XVI named you Secretary of the Pontifical Council for the Family. At the same time, you

were ordained bishop by Cardinal Bertone, the current Cardinal Sec-
retary of State, at Saint Peter's in Rome, on December 12 of that year.

J.L. Yes.

Could you tell us in what manner the fact of being a bishop
defines your mission, its color and type? You are a bishop without a
doubt because you hold an important post. But are you not a bishop
especially in order to fulfill this function?

J.L. I would say that what is most important, and addresses
this question at a personal level, is the fact of being enrolled in
succession to the Apostles. The Apostles were called together;
they formed an apostolic college. You understand once you
are a bishop that being called to the episcopacy and being ordained a bishop enrolls you among the number of those who
continue the apostolic college: It is the college of bishops. This
is not at all theoretical but is very practical: You are connected
to the entire group of the other bishops, coming from all cor-
ners of the earth. There is a very fraternal dimension present
there. From the start, you are inserted into a collegiality, and
you understand that very quickly. Something is there that precedes you and joins you together in a manner you had never
imagined.

But is it not the simple fact of belonging to a "corps"?

J.L. No! You are inserted into a "corps," but in a living way.
The other bishops are not colleagues. They are brothers in the
episcopacy. The vision that you have of the Church evolves
necessarily in a loving sense, a sense of respect for callings and
missions. There are numerous and diverse callings within the

Church, in dioceses that are very different from one another, in the particular churches within the bosoms of varied cultures and countries, and finally in ecclesial services that are very different from one another.

And the fact of being in Rome equally characterizes your ministry?

J.L. This episcopal dimension completes and colors itself by this experience of being in Rome with the successor to the first of the Apostles. There is a new bond that is created, a bond of fraternity in the episcopacy with the Pope, with all that you can imagine in terms of deference, respect, and submission to the successor of Peter and the extraordinary mission that is his.

Concerning this vital bond with Peter and his successor, is it not felt more acutely here in Rome?

J.L. I was not named as the residential bishop of a diocese, and in this sense I have had more of an opportunity to allow that aspect to develop, necessarily. The service that today is mine concerns itself with all of the churches. It is a universal *service*, in the entire geographic range of the term. Of course, I perceive all of its pastoral dimensions by the fact that I travel a lot: I visit numerous dioceses; I participate as a bishop in numerous celebrations; and I meet with seminarians, religious, and associations of Christian families and married couples. But from the start, it is this experience of being immersed straightaway into an episcopal college that is a living reality.

In what concretely does your work consist, your ministry of today?

J.L. From a classical perspective, just as with the other dicasteries, we receive at the Council for the Family around six hundred bishops each year during their *ad limina* visit. It is the occasion for them to provide information on the situation in their diocese and also to express their pastoral concerns. The dialogue is often profound, and these meetings create bonds with numerous pastors across different countries. We also receive all of the associations of families and married couples who desire to meet with us. We are in relationship with approximately four hundred associations in the world. We thus have daily contact with laypeople, for families are composed above all of laypeople! We also meet with different groups who wish to visit us: seminarians, university professors, agents of family pastoral ministry, groups of pilgrims who accompany their bishop, and political officials. The Council organizes colloquia and congresses as well, and tries to bring together different associations that are engaged in pastoral work concerning the family and life. We also publish several things, such as the *Lexicon of Ambiguous and Controversial Terms on the Family, Life, and Ethical Questions*, the French translation of which appeared in 2005,[7] and which has been translated into eleven languages in all, as well as the *Enchiridion of the Family*. The Council edits a journal as well, *Familia et Vita*. We try to help the episcopal conferences, through the mediation of the apostolic nunciatures, on the juridical questions concerning international organizations as well as some pieces of national legislation. Currently, we are in the middle of preparing a *Pastoral Manual of Preparation for Marriage* (*Vade mecum*). Finally, every three years we organize a

---

7 Pontifical Council for the Family, *Lexicon: Ambiguous and Debatable Terms Regarding Family, Life and Ethical Questions*. Front Royal, Virginia: Human Life International, 2006.

World Meeting of Families. The next Meeting will take place in Milan in the presence of the Holy Father, from May 30 through June 3, 2012. We have two or three meetings each month with our counterparts from Milan for the preparation of this event, at which it is foreseen that more than one million people will come together, as was the case in Valencia and in Mexico City.

Do you have to get involved on all fronts both ad intra *and* ad extra?

J.L. Yes, but *ad extra* we can only speak to people who want to listen to us. It is a very important aspect of our work. We have contact with politicians, international institutions, and nongovernmental organizations. For example, I had the occasion of meeting the European Parliament in Brussels in September 2010. Finally, we go into the universities and regularly are invited into international colloquia that are not strictly Christian. We participate in scientific congresses within the spheres of the family, bioethics, sexuality, and the promotion and defense of life.

Ad intra, we do the same thing, but for Christian groups; faculties of philosophy, theology, and the humanities. We meet groups of bishops, and at times I participate in sessions for the formation of bishops. Recently in Bogotá, Colombia, the presidency of the Council for the Family organized a workweek with CELAM (Conference of Bishops of Latin America) on different questions related to marriage and the family. All of the officials concerned with family pastoral work from the countries of South and Central America participated there.

The entirety of our activities are conducted under the authority of the president of the Council for the Family. Cardinal Ennio Antonelli is the current president.

Ad extra, we recall your speech in 2007 before the French presidential election concerning conscientious objection and its extension to doctors, but also to nurses and pharmacists on the sale of abortifacients.

J.L. Yes, this communication had some repercussions. It was during the congress organized by the Pontifical Academy for Life and was open to all. Recently, I was asked by the journal *Politique Internationale* to write an article on health and organ donation. This nonreligious journal desired to hear a voice from the Church. In that edition, there were contributions from international personalities coming from different viewpoints, for example from the Secretary General of the United Nations, the director of the World Health Organization, and others. Consequently, it is an all-out action to which we are called, sometimes in unexpected ways. Inevitably, we must move about often.

Your ministry is thus one of real involvement. On this subject, Benedict XVI encourages all of the officials in the heart of the Church:

I think that courage is one of the chief qualities that a bishop and Curia head has to have nowadays. One aspect of this courage is the refusal to bow to the dictate of opinions but, rather, to act on the basis of what one inwardly knows is right, even when it causes annoyance. And of course the candidates have to be people who have qualities of intellect, professionalism, and humanity, so that they can also lead and draw others into a close-knit community.[8]

---

8 Pope Benedict XVI, *Light of the World: The Pope, the Church, and the Signs of the Times: A Conversation with Peter Seewald.* San Francisco: Ignatius, 2010, p. 85.

How do you react when faced with difficulties in communication, notably on the topic of the family, in our contemporary world?

J.L. There are difficulties that we, like all men of good will, have to confront. Each man of good will cannot but be challenged by the questioning of values as fundamental as marriage and the family. The institution of the family is a reality that, during the centuries, has structured our societies, not only in the West but also across a very large number of cultures. And yet, this institution is contested today. It has not only been given a pounding juridically by the development of legislative initiatives, but also in a more immediately concrete manner by the choice that more and more people make not to integrate the desire to found a family within their own life plan.

However, we cannot limit ourselves to observing things that are going badly. How often we speak only of things that are going badly! But in reality, we discover many things that go well, if we bother to broaden our gaze! Many people still live a love that flourishes at home and in a family. Within the nature of man and woman are experiences written very deeply in their hearts, experiences that John Paul II called essential, elementary, or fundamental, the foremost of which is the desire to love and to be loved. When someone is animated by this desire, particularly during adolescence, he can't imagine that the love he desires profoundly, and which he begins perhaps to experience thanks to an amorous encounter, could be destined to end. As Angelo Scola has remarked, no adolescent exists who is able to say, "I love such-and-such a guy" or "I love such-and-such a girl" and, within the same minute, "I admit that in a few months or years I will be able to stop loving" him or her. If he follows such a line of reasoning, it means that he does not love the other. He has not experienced

love. He experiences something thrilling at the psychological
level, but this love remains immature; love carries in principle all
of the sufferings, disillusions, difficulties, and obstacles of the future. What absolutely must be encouraged is that each person be
able to observe himself going very deeply to the heart of his desire.
When you meet someone else and say, "I love you," you would like
for this love to last forever. The two things are linked. It's as much
as to say, "I cannot envision my life without you."

Is it a tremendous undertaking?

J.L. It is a tremendous undertaking because it is precisely the
action of educators, of parents and also Christians, to bring into
focus this richness of desire that is written deeply in man's heart.
Only then will it become possible to discover how much the
institution of the family and openness to life truly correspond to
the nature of this desire.

To return to the question, when you work in service of the
family, you are obliged to be attentive to what happens at the
social level, in relation to the common good, legislation, politics
of the state and international organizations, because this falls
within your competence. There are moments where it must be
stated clearly: It is not permissible for the institution of the family to be trivialized by comparing it with all forms of relationship
between two persons; or for a child to be deprived of the possibility of being born within a stable and harmonious setting that
is assured only by the loving presence of a father and a mother.
For us, it is a moral demand tied to the responsibility that the
Holy Father has entrusted to us, one that includes the care of
persons, their happiness, and service to the truth; as well as care
for the rights of God, which one often forgets. God has rights
over us. It could be formulated otherwise, saying: *the care for the*

rights of the Creator, which enters into the task of the pastor. He must live it serenely, knowing that each day brings its fruits, its labor, its trials, but also its hopes.

One must not be obsessed with the negative aspects.

J.L. In no case. Love is always good news, and it is good news that is always accessible. There is no need to be rich or poor, to be in a good or bad situation, to be famous or unknown in order to attain this kind of extraordinary experience that is love. This love that opens us to others takes several forms. There is of course conjugal love, but there are equally other profound expressions of love; they make us grow and are also experiences of transcendence. The love of solidarity toward persons who are materially or spiritually in need, toward those who suffer from loneliness or who live in exile, is a love within which God is acting. The love through which a person is driven to establish a family with the person whom he sees he cannot live without, is a love where God does not stop being present. It is the same thing concerning filial, maternal, and paternal love: They are the very expressions of who man is as a child of God. You can develop these abilities to love, while going to meet others in a deep communion. One must not be pessimistic but instead must be fundamentally realistic: No person, no legislation, no media, no ideology can shake the sovereign freedom of a heart that has decided to love.

Saint-Exupéry said that a person cannot be responsible and desperate at the same time.

J.L. Exactly. All ecclesial (and also civil) responsibility demands the faith that our responsible action may bear fruit. It assumes hope as well.

You are a moral theologian in your training and in the field. You pay attention to what people tell you, to their objections, contradictions, even sufferings and joys. And I would like to conclude this presentation by returning to the method that you seem to be implementing: You are pragmatic, you see things as they are. I take up again the title of one of your conferences, "The Christian Experience of the Family." You say, "The family is a concrete reality before being the subject matter of a philosophical choice or a political opinion." This manner of addressing questions, without evading reflection, seems to us to be able to touch persons and make them reflect. In that regard, are you not fully in the line of John Paul II, and, returning to a French Christian philosopher, Maurice Blondel?

J.L. As you know, beginning from experience characterizes a personalist approach that, incidentally, is not exclusively that of French personalism. There is indeed a personalist current of German origin tied to the phenomenological tradition. Max Scheler is cited often due to the impact he had on the thought of Karol Wojtyła; but let us think also of the great German thinkers such as Romano Guardini, Dietrich von Hildebrand, Edith Stein, or even Ferdinand Ebner or Martin Buber. It isn't about idolizing experience as such, but rather taking the real as the starting point. At its heart, within the context of the family and at the level of personal life, it is an expression of this approach that consists in starting from the real, from the *res*. One does not begin with a principle that then is applied; but, in light of what has been revealed to us concerning the truth of man, of his relationships, of the world, of the Creator, and looking at the concrete life of man, one can contemplate this truth that he is called to life. What's at stake is a truth that we don't first confront with our own experience, but with the truth revealed by and in Christ, and it also involves the truth concerning man that is accessible to reason. "Only Christ knows what is within man," the Second Vatican Council tells us.

On the matter of love, experience is primary. One does not ask himself one beautiful day, "Oh, what is love?" No. Rather: "How does it come to me? How does it happen in me? Why do I think endlessly about this person, and why is this thought filling me with joy?" Why then does the question of God pose itself to us in terms of love given and love received? When you teach on these matters, what you say first of all involves all men of good will, but also finds itself in agreement with the nature of the Christian life. Christian life is not an ideology, a current of opinion, a theory, a mathematical axiom, a prejudice. Christian life is primarily the experience of God who reveals Himself to man. It is the experience that men have of this God who reveals Himself by loving us. It cannot be invented.

All of the great Christian thinkers, the Gospel writers, Saint Paul, the Fathers of the Church, the martyrs, the great theologians such as Saint Augustine, the mystical saints like Saint Francis of Assisi, as well as the saints of today like Mother Teresa, who is a great spiritual master, are all part of the reality of who God is and what He has done in their lives. God allows Himself to be contemplated. He exists before we contemplate Him! Yes, experience precedes analysis or the *a priori* explanations that man is tempted to develop.

The foremost reality is God?

J.L. Yes. And the first act of man is an act that is, as it were, preconscious: The reality of life already expresses the relation that man has with God. The first thing that we are called to do, we do not even know we are doing: We live. Thus, there is a connection to God that has been given right away by the

Creator. Afterward, experience develops; at a given moment we are born, we discover a world, we distance ourselves from our mother, we learn to say "I," we discover other people, we grow up and begin to reflect upon ourselves. Life—the experience of life—is a profound teaching because it is a teaching that God gives us from the outset. You can manipulate all you like, but no one ever decided to live! Others perhaps have decided for you, and more! When they brought you into the world, they did not know the person you would be! We have to have a contemplative gaze: God is the first reality, He preexists men, He is the eternal present. The man who contemplates Him can draw profound lessons from the actions he is led to live through the central experience of the good and of love. Man cannot live without love. If he does, it's an infirmity . . . It's the great, the only infirmity.

TWO

Engagement:
Giving One's Faith

Pierre and Véronique Sanchez: *Marriage preparation varies from one country to another, and even from one parish to the next. Could you speak to us about it?*

Bishop Jean Laffitte: In order not to have the wrong perspective, one must understand that when the Church speaks of "marriage preparation," she means primarily and above all "preparation to receive the sacrament of marriage." She emphasizes an event that is a Christian event. For, to take up an image from *Gaudium et Spes*, at the moment when the couple marries, Christ comes to meet them in order to dwell with them for the entire length of their lives. The Church holds to a conviction: From the moment the bride and groom marry and receive the sacrament of marriage, this sacrament, far from being limited to the moment of the celebration, is given for the whole of their common life.

One may think about, search for, and deepen the terms used to express this reality. The Church has never found a better term than that of *covenant*. Covenant returns us to the Biblical tradition. The term *covenant* allows us to render an account

of the fact that an indissoluble relationship is established between two persons who unite their destiny; they are allied. But
covenant implies the relationship that God maintains with the
Church. God made a covenant with the people of Israel; Christ
sealed a covenant with men by handing over His life, operating
thus as the Head of this Body that is the Church. The category
of *covenant* gives you on the one hand this horizontal union of
man and woman who unite themselves together—this is the
covenant of the spouses—but at the same time, this horizontal
union points to the covenant that God has with each one of
them. It is the meeting of two kinds of covenant: the covenant
of the spouses, and God's covenant with each one of them and
with the two together.

This is a Christian event. The difficulty with which you
are familiar comes from the fact that many people demand the
sacrament of marriage from the Church while totally misunderstanding what the sacrament signifies. Unfortunately, sometimes people are indifferent to what God can do, to the way He
is able to act, and to the reasons why He enters into contact with
the married couple. The Church is concerned with showing the
consistency of the sacrament of marriage, which is important.
The Church can only approach marriage from a profoundly realistic perspective. Taking this into consideration is the purpose
of preparation: We need to be aware of the ignorance—or of a
very partial or incomplete knowledge, lacking in longing, desire,
or enthusiasm—that typifies numerous young people wanting
to get married. Many of these young people unfortunately ex-
hibit this distinctive trait. In order to attain her objective, the
Church tries to demonstrate a certain number of the inherent
attributes of human love that apply to all relationships involving authentic love, even when the persons—through no fault

of their own—do not have a lived, personal knowledge of the teaching of God and of Christ.

When there is authentic love between a man and a woman, different things happen that the fiancés have an interest in knowing. I will give you an example concerning the question of the indissolubility of love. Often people think: "Church forbids divorce and says that marriage is indissoluble. In fact, outside of the Church, it is possible to divorce and even to do so several times. Therefore, indissolubility is a particular demand of the Church." But this is not at all the case. The Church considers a marriage valid, free, authentic, unable to be dissolved, not in order to establish a rule that would impose itself from the outside—a sort of moral norm that would be proper to it—but because indissolubility is demanded by the very nature of love. The Church does not express rigorism here, or a lack of realism, forgetting the difficulty of life today or that dangers, including emotional ones, are ever present. No! The love between a man and a woman takes its complete and mature form in the gift that each makes of himself to the other, and this gift can only be irrevocable. Why is this gift irrevocable? A gift is not a loan. One does not say: "I am giving myself to you for five years—that's a good period of time—but I rule out that it may be for ten years, or twenty, or thirty!"

It is not a voidable contract, as with an insurance company!

J.L. No. It is a gift for always. This gift will create a reality: a conjugal communion that, when it is expressed and lived out in its fullness, has as a possible result the eventual coming into existence of a new human life, if God wills it and if nature makes it possible. One has a love here that is a creator of life! It is a tremendous thing. Of course, it only comes about in a way that is subordinate to the immediate creative action of God. But without such cooperation, without this procreation with God, there is no human life.

You'll hear that many things can be done now concerning the generation of life. Of course, one need refer only to the multiple procedures of artificial procreation. In this case, however, man separates the gift of human life from any sexual expression of human love. One can manipulate things, but at the price of removing this characteristic trait of love. Within the natural order, there is no possibility for a human being to come into existence other than by way of this amorous encounter, following the total gift that the man and woman make of themselves to one other. The sacrament of marriage sanctifies, elevates, and adds a particular firmness to this reality of the indissolubility of love. It gives this gift: Christ comes to encounter the spouses, in order to remain with them forever.

If Christ unites himself sacramentally with the married couple, He will not abandon His covenant on the pretext that the spouses have decided to divorce. That would make no sense. For this reason, if the sacrament is valid then it cannot cease to be so. The Church has neither the possibility nor the power to say the contrary: "This sacrament was valid; I declare that it is invalid." Why? Because the sacrament is a work of God. Christ has raised human love to the dignity of a sacrament. It is not the norm of the Church that did so. The norm of the Church codified it and made it explicit, of course, and gave the sacrament its form and canonical rules, but she did not create it. Let us remember the words of Christ in His conversation with the Pharisees, "From the beginning, it was not so," when He referred to the bill of repudiation of a spouse that Moses had allowed (Matt. 19).

The Church wants to bring into focus that preparation for the sacrament of marriage means entering little by little into the understanding of this mystery, of what the fiancés are living, and of the mystery of God. In the document that we are preparing, we mention the way in which God sanctifies human love and also the manner in which young people live out human love. The document will present the means of preparing for the sacrament in an appropriate manner. The Church thus presents what should be involved in any serious preparation, not only in terms of immediate preparation just before the sacrament, but also the preparation during engagement as well as more remote preparation. I would almost like to say that one prepares himself for marriage starting from the day of one's birth. From childhood on, man experiences a love that requires on our part a maturation of our bodily, affective, and spiritual being. The Church takes into consideration the entirety of these dimensions concerning man and woman.

"Fiancés who live together," observed Alain Quilici, *"are objectively no longer fiancés. They already form a couple. Their life is already conjugal, even if they cannot say yet that they are married."*[9] *Wouldn't one of the major problems of our contemporary Western societies have to be mentioned here: that of loneliness, of the fundamental incapacity to be alone, which leads young people to get together in an anarchic manner, without an awareness that the fear of loneliness and the incapacity of coming to terms with it are the greatest obstacles to the blossoming of love?*

J.L. I completely agree with this diagnosis, which consists of seeing within the pattern of getting together—as happens very

9 Alain Quilici, *Les Fiançailles.* Fayard-Le Sarment, 1993, p. 39.

frequently, for example, with students—the incapacity to accept the demands of a certain solitude. Each person knows that solitude can bring joys and trials, difficulties, as well as desire for the company of others, but at the same time solitude is a necessary place where the person is confronted with the present, with his own actions, with his future, where this is being constructed. Despite this, there is a fear of remaining alone. A lot of people are not able to be alone for ten minutes; they absolutely must enter into a relationship, telephoning, speaking, sending messages.

But your question makes me think that, when John Paul II was examining the mystery of human love in his Wednesday catecheses, he began from the experience of Adam's original solitude. He recognized within man's heart the desire to come out of solitude. Yet man may only come out of solitude on the condition that it has first been confronted and not avoided. Therefore, there are a great number of young people who start living together without having the least project for the future. It is a kind of arrangement, an act without reflection. You are gratified by the other's company, you achieve immediate and proximate satisfaction from living together, from living your own affectivity and exercising your sexuality. However, you face neither the future nor the present nor anything of the kind, and you do not truly establish yourself. When young people live together in this way, they are not able to build themselves in truth. Why? Because the fact of their being together does not correspond to a gift. When this cohabitation stops being satisfying for one or the other, or both of them, they decide to end it. There is no need to endure this union that is unsatisfactory. People think that they are free, so they discontinue this relationship, perhaps before engaging in another. *I am free again*, or so think those who put an end to this type of union—those who, it may be said in passing, seem to express that they were not free before. And they leave again . . . To unite together cannot be a simple "collage." It must be a gift, a path that engages our spiritual faculties and not simply our affective desire. In reality, cohabitation is connected to a weakness of heart, of the soul, of the will. In any case, the young people will meet loneliness again sooner or later, and in every case, they will meet loneliness yet again when they move on from their old life to a new one. There is something foundational in all solitude: When we are born, we are alone, we are separated from our mothers. I really think that solitude is a structuring experience throughout all of life.

The second thing is the misreading of what a common life actually is. It is often seen as a fusion: We are together because we are well. There is no consideration of the freedom of the other that could want to say: "I am preparing myself, I am preparing myself for you. It is for you that right now I wish to live alone, in order to be better for you tomorrow!" A young person of good will can understand that very deeply. How many times do we want to live out a joy and prepare ourselves to live it? We await it because it is not yet there; we caress it through our imagination, in our sensitivity. "Oh, in a month I will meet such-and-such a friend, and I will participate in such-and-such an event." We await happy things, for we do not have them immediately. There is an experience of desire that finds itself building up, becoming stronger, precisely within a solitude that has been accepted and taken on.

I will add one final thought that is the fruit of my personal reflections. I think that, within the issue of cohabitation, there is a very great injustice committed in relation to the woman. I am now convinced of this. When two young people start living together, when this common life ends—sometimes at the end of one year but perhaps more, up to ten years—the two do not start all over again, each to his own way as if nothing had been. The man will suffer, but he will return back to normal more easily. The woman has given the man something of herself that is unique. She will find that she has already profoundly given the gift of herself to someone who will be able to say to her: "We had a good time together, but I'm moving on now." There is suffering within the woman. How can the woman give herself over a second time, a third time, with the same expectancy? You really have to be living in a masculine egotism to imagine for one second that a young woman necessarily will have the drive, the desire, and the enthusiasm to give herself to a man whom she loves a second, a third, or a fifth time! There is total ignorance of the difference that exists at the affective level between a masculine and feminine psychology and affectivity. To me, cohabitation is an injustice with respect to the woman. She lets go of much more of herself than the man does if this cohabitation has to end. It is so in the majority of cases. It seems to me that only the mothers of families are conscious of it.

Often people live together and think as well about preparing for an eventual marriage. They are mistaken, and all the more so as it is known that there is a greater proportion of divorces among people who have lived together than among people who did not cohabit before marriage, an enormous difference in proportion. Cohabitation weakens and deteriorates the capability to face difficulties later. Why? When you cohabit, if there is a major difficulty, then the answer is simple: You can put the cohabitation to an end. Thus the difficulty is contravened; it disappears momentarily, but it has not been resolved. And often without knowing, you set off again with this difficulty within you. It will reappear sooner or later.

I terminate my telephone contract and change my telephone company . . .

J.L. You terminate it, but the problem only seems to be resolved. Today, unfortunately, when a serious problem poses itself after you have contracted a marriage, you are in the same psychological mindset and are tempted to apply the same procedure. The number of divorces in marriages that follow several years of cohabitation is very high within the first five years of wedlock. Moreover, the longer the couple has cohabited, the greater the fragility of the future couple.

People ask me: "What do you think of cohabitation? Why would one not have the right to cohabit?" I respond: "Nobody will stop you from cohabiting if you wish it!" I often tell young people: "What are you putting into this cohabitation?" As is always the case, any young woman who is in love contributes more to this choice than the man does. That's just how it is, and psychologists know it. All the while, they act as if nothing were happening; they live together. When the young man leaves, he absolutely does not worry himself over "the one whom he leaves for dead," permit me to use this expression. The ordeal of separation may be painful for the young man as well, but he will get over it more easily. The tracks always remain, especially in the case of a separation after a love expressed through a profound union; but these marks impact the woman much more in her flesh and in her affectivity, inside her heart. Moreover, the young woman who has lived together in cohabitation often has been asked to take a contraceptive over the course of many years, for the comfort of her cohabiting partner, and to put up every possible obstacle against becoming a mother. These are not neutral experiences.

You are a feminist!

J.L. But of course! The Church is feminist in the Christian sense of the term, that is to say, she has the greatest respect for the dignity of the human person, and thus for the woman. There is a Christian feminism, and we need not be afraid to say it. Such a vision, however, has nothing to do with the negative ideology of femininity. When a young man loves a young woman, the respect that he shows her is the best gauge to measure the authenticity of his loving sentiment. When someone loves, he respects.

Does the spread of cohabitation before marriage not manifest, within the heart of the institution that is the family, the presence of a snake that bites its own tail: Parents who love each other as they are able but without the help and richness of God's love, and who then tear away from each other, leave in their wake serious emotional gaps in their children's history that then open up upon the threshold of their adult life into an affective immaturity, one that is profoundly harmful to their desire for love?

J.L. Yes. It is a fact noted from observation and at times from experience. If the parents have put up the show of a couple without reciprocal care, without a common enthusiasm, if they have seemed to live their lives together as a common misfortune because it was the convention of a certain era, then it is certain that the very image of marriage could be deformed and could have exerted its influence upon people's resilience, such that some prefer to live out a strong but short-lived experience, rather than to involve themselves in something that the couple mistakenly thinks will make them suffer for all of their lives.

So this accurate observation renders marriage preparation

necessary, a process that is not limited to the preparation of a ceremony but which is also an in-depth dialogue with the spouses, and a verification—with due discretion and respect for the intimacy of each spouse—of what the two are expecting from marriage, of their idea of love. How do they think of integrating the dimension of pardon and reconciliation, for example? I insist: Within marriage—and small things are included—there must be an ordinary practice of reconciliation. There is no need to imagine abominable offenses. During such preparation, one also must address the question of knowing how two persons envision their common life, and how to make their love come alive throughout the length of their daily conjugal life. It is good for them to talk about it. This requires time for preparation, a time of engagement that is reasonable. Such preparation is not an inquisition, or a new norm; it is also not a weight upon the shoulders of those who sincerely desire to get married with simplicity; but it is truly an occasion for serious reflection. One takes seriously the beautiful and holy desire of two persons to get married, and to do so in the Lord, as an act that does not exclude God from their shared life.

Within this context, among the candidates for Christian marriage, there are more and more couples in civil unions. What is the position of the Church in the face of this phenomenon—or concerning a couple's life before marriage? One has the impression that the Church is slipping, only too happy to have some couples who present themselves to her . . .

J.L. This is an awful thing to say, but I understand fully why the question is asked in these terms, because it is one that must be asked of pastors, of each priest and bishop. They must ask themselves: "Do I provide this treasure of the sacrament of

Christ in good condition to these young people? Or do I put my head in the sand? Do I not want to know what they have done beforehand and what they want to do afterward? I will give them the sacrament and wash my hands of the fate—perhaps biased—to which they are about to commit themselves."

For a healthy and authentic preparation of the couple, I think there has to be a personalized discussion with the priest, and eventually between a mentor couple and each of the two fiancés, though not necessarily always together, but individually. And this for the reasons that we already have mentioned: What has been lived between them has not left the same marks on each of them. On both sides, why would a couple who lives together wish to marry? It is because they are experimenting that they have not enjoyed access to the complete happiness and joy they could have. For today, who are the people living in a state of cohabitation or common-law marriage, and who want to get married in the Church? For what motives—out of religious, family, or civil convention? Often they tell you in a clumsy way: It is not the same thing to get married in the Church. They do not manage to say what it is, but in their eyes, there is something greater in the action of getting married in the Church: They sense that they are getting married before God.

The preparation must thus be articulated: To accompany the couples and, for that to happen, to meet with them and love them. The priest must have an interest in their happiness. He cannot prepare people indifferently. If I prepare engaged couples, and it happens that I must refuse due to lack of availability, I am part stakeholder and desire deeply that they be happy. So, I am led to prepare them with all my heart as a priest, within my limits, but with all my heart. I will not carry out a formal act rapidly without taking the necessary time, nor will I content myself with merely making them sign forms of declaration of intention! Rather, I will see who is in front of me. I will want to know how they met! The priest must love people. If he does not love them, he is not a stakeholder and is indifferent to what they have lived previously. If he does love them, he will not carry out an inquisition, but he will listen to them. He can introduce them to the Christian concept of love, he prays for them and with them and leads them to pray. If he does not introduce the engaged couple into an experience of prayer, I do not know where they are headed! I find it insane that people are prepared over the course of months for the sacrament of marriage and may not even have had one occasion to pray, that nobody invites them to pray and to entrust their happiness to God, or even to ask what God wants for them! This preparation must be a spiritual event. It is not only accompaniment at the psychological or social level, or out of good will or friendship on the part of the priest or the accompanying couple. The fiancés must feel loved and be led to Christ. There is then an opening of the heart that takes place, and then there can be space for the grace of Christ. We have to believe it.

You give the ideal. But in reality, do you think it is doable?

J.L. Speaking of the ideal does not mean speaking of something unrealistic or inaccessible. We recently celebrated the pope of marriage, John Paul II, who was beatified several weeks ago. When he would speak of conjugal holiness, of the holiness of priests, he would speak of it in such a manner that he had to face this objection: Is this not the very peak of conjugal mysticism? Or the mysticism of the priestly ideal . . . or Polish mysticism, people would add? Ultimately, today, who was the realist? It was he, not those who were criticizing him. He caught hold in a realistic manner of the call to holiness that was his, and which he identified as belonging to all people and to all of the baptized.

To be a saint—it is an ideal, but not an imaginary one. It is the goal of all existence. The great sadness of a man, of a Christian, should be to discover that he is not a saint. There is something that tugs at our heart: a nostalgia—not at all melancholic but positive—that motivates us. Oh, if we were able to be saints! John Paul II saw that, and we see the results today! What would we say of Mother Teresa! When we read her spiritual writings, we see well that the goal upon which she was focused seemed inaccessible. In reality, she already was at the point of arriving at the goal; she was a saint!

We must say time and time again that there is no gradation in God's calling. God calls us to be his friends, the friends of Christ. By definition, saintliness is friendship with Christ. When Christ offers his friendship, he does not say: I offer to you a friendship of the first degree; go to Mass each Sunday, we will see each other again in eternity, and you will have the grace of a happy death! No. Christ says to each one of us: I want to love you, and I want your love. There are differences between persons, because there are differences in the responses. But within the calling of God Himself, this is not the case. There can be exceptional destinies connected to divine election, but God does not cheat man: He never offers man a love that is second-best. There is a great deal of seriousness in the call to holiness, and I think that when one presents it to future spouses who are of good will (something I always emphasize), they can only be touched and struck by this proposal that is made to them. Afterward, they will have to think on it often, come back to it, speak of it, be accompanied. There is no marriage preparation without a concern for accompanying young people after marriage, during the years that follow. Preparation for marriage does not stop on the day of the celebration! You have parishes where there are no activities for couples, where nothing is proposed to families or to young couples. When this is the case, there is no possibility in them of a well-nourished spiritual life. People who are motivated will look elsewhere, in places where their desire to grow closer to Christ is taken seriously. But this should be the concern of all of the Church, of all priests and bishops, to offer to young people who live the mystery of love in truth the possibility to fortify themselves, to grow stronger and to thrive in joy and in hope.

For those who desire to consecrate themselves to God, a time of preparation also exists, a probationary period before final vows for religious, or before ordination for clergy, as is the case for fiancés before marriage. Is it possible to establish a parallel between the two? Is it not a privileged time in the desert?

J.L. When you say the word *desert*, you are putting the question of solitude back on the table in another way. What is the desert? It is a meeting with God in solitude and silence. Actually, a time in the desert is necessary—one of reflection, of introspection, of getting right with God, of walking with Him, of growing stronger in purpose. In effect, there are two principle states of life: marriage, and consecration in celibacy with a view to the religious life or the ordained ministry, or finally to consecrated lay life. Actually, these different callings may converge in a single path: God's call to holiness, to which man and woman may respond in different ways. In either case—that is, in marriage or consecrated celibacy—we have the response to a calling that is aroused in us by an object of love. In marriage, the offer that God gives us of His love passes through the mediation of the beloved person, of the future bride or groom. In religious life, there

is a kind of immediacy: a mediation of belonging to God that
is expressed by all of the ascetic practices proper to religious life,
but a belonging that will be real throughout all of religious
life. Consequently, men and women are not able to prepare
themselves completely for religious life. Rather, they are perfected in it throughout their existence in the same manner that
spouses are perfected through marriage over the course of their
lives as husband and wife. One prepares to embrace the religious
life; one prepares to embrace conjugal life. However, the two of
them proceed intrinsically from the same dynamism: respond-
ing to the calling and the offer of God to follow Him and to love
Him in truth. How can we love Him in truth? I would say: Do
not cheat in love. There are falls, infidelities, discouragements,
even trials and deceptions. Happily, though, all these difficulties
never happen at the same time!

Step by step!

J.L. Exactly. As one goes along, day after day. A question
can arise today, but today does not bring the answer to tomorrow's difficulty. God's grace is present for today, and it is this
certainty that carries us. With the prolonging of life expectancy,
you now have couples who celebrate their sixtieth anniversary,
or even their seventieth anniversary of conjugal life; the same
goes for religious life.

Last week, we met a monk of Cîteaux who entered the abbey in
1939 and who radiated joy and peace.

J.L. That's very understandable. Fidelity generates joy. Fidelity is rooted in the present moment of each day. When couples—
or religious or priests—arrive at an anniversary, they can say

to God: Lord, you were with me all the days of my life over the course of sixty years! It's tremendous. Fidelity is the joy of a love that lasts. It also entails a moral commitment and profoundly has to do with the joy of a love that lasts, one that never dies but rather abides.

Concerning the vocation of priests and religious, there is a discernment process involving the bishop and other leaders. What about in marriage? Who is able to discern?

J.L. It is important to see that the fundamental spiritual demands of these two states of life of which we have spoken may be considered to be the same, but their respective concrete demands are not. In effect, marriage corresponds to a natural longing within the heart of every human being to unite with a person of the opposite sex, and to perpetuate this union through filiation, through fatherhood and motherhood. This corresponds to the very large majority of men and women.

In matters that concern religious and priestly life, there is a path that is a challenge in comparison to the intelligibility of the world. How can we understand that a well-balanced young man or woman—one who has a heart, a body, affectivity, and a desire for fertility—could accept a renunciation of these obvious and directly perceptible joys in daily life, for a love that one knows is demanding, that will not stop being a purification day after day and thus will require continual renunciations? When you are destined to become a priest, for example, you do not renounce marriage only on the day that you enter seminary or, in a definitive manner, on the day when you are ordained a deacon. It's about a choice that you renew, as it were, each day.

There is, therefore, a difference that we must bring into focus: If God calls someone to marry, He calls him to become a great saint in the state of marriage; the same is true if He should call him to consecrated life or the ministerial priesthood. Religious life, just like priestly life, is a state of life that requires renunciations and contains great joys but also sacrifices, such as for example the solitude of which we were speaking a short time ago. All of the congregations or communities of the world do not make up for the need of the consecrated person from time to time to confront the fact that he is alone before his Lord. Will he converse with Him, listen to Him, tell Him that he loves Him, or will he be unfaithful to his solitude by way of distractions?

To prepare himself for this state of life, it is normal that he have a long time of preparation, of being put to the test; and that there is not only a spiritual discernment of the reality of God's calling, but also of his capacity to respond to it, as much as human weakness permits him to discern this.

Why isn't there discernment in marriage? That is the question. Very naturally, the Christian who lives a Christian life necessarily is called to discern between the different desires that fill his or her heart. When the desire that dwells there is to share life for all time with such-and-such a young woman or such-and-such a young man, the person naturally will ask the question: Is this truly the precise happiness and the precise form that God wants for me and for my life, for the fulfillment of my vocation and thus for my happiness? Of course, God leaves man free to choose to marry such-and-such a person. However, the Christian life is made up all day long of a mass of small discernments. Why would people who get married for always not entrust to God the intention that He shed light upon what is good for them? In reality, persons who pray do so naturally. There is a given moment where peace increases in the heart, along with joy, hope in the future, and a desire to have children with this woman or that man. When a young, twenty-year-old man comes to see me and says, "I assure you, this is really the one . . . She is fantastic, and I would like to introduce her to you," during the conversation at an opportune moment I am brought to ask him, "Is she truly the one, and not another, with whom you would like to have children later?" The response is often very clear: "Yes, she and no other!" In that response is a very strong sign. Thus, there is a discernment that one carries out with regard to people who love you or who help you, and also through trusting conversation with God in prayer! Why would future spouses not pray for God to enlighten them, to show them the desirable moment? Why? Because nobody has told them to do so.

The time of preparation is very important for future spouses. We are focusing our pastoral marriage preparation manual on three moments: the remote preparation that begins in childhood, the proximate preparation that is engagement, and the preparation immediately prior to marriage. This path of preparation demands discernment at all of its stages.

The word engagement *and the word* trust, *as well as the word* faith, *are from the same family. It would seem that the disrepute into which family, fidelity, and chastity have fallen during the "night preceding the battle," which constitutes the time of marriage preparation, may be linked with the phenomenon of "unbelief," of which Cardinal Poupard spoke.*[10] *The loss of faith in God seems inseparable from the loss of trust in a lasting love rooted in fidelity. What do you think?*

J.L. Trust is the joyous and most childlike form—in the good sense of the term—of faith. Faith, the *fides*, refers as much

---

10 See Cardinal Paul Poupard, *La Décroyance*, interviews with Véronique Dufief. L'Echelle de Jacob, Collection Visages, 2012.

to that in which we believe—and the content of articles of the faith, if you will—as to trust. In several romance languages, the same word is used. In trust, there is a double movement: the fact of confiding oneself to someone, and that of having trust in him. The two things are connected. One must know that trust is the most structuring element of the human personality. The first moral experience that a human being has is the trust he has toward his mother, who offers him complete security. He then separates from her, and he must come to terms with another face, the paternal figure of authority who steps in. He discovers that he is not alone in having rights to his mother and must integrate this father figure. This phenomenon will be accomplished in him when he has understood that his father and mother together form an object of love and trust. The fundamental ethical experience is this: He believes that his parents are worthy of trust. He discovers that his parents want the best for him and always look out for his good. He will grow up with a little responsibility, then with more important responsibility. He will be used to not lying, not concealing, not hiding; telling the truth to his parents. His parents will correct him if he does wrong, if he has acted badly; but in his parents, who are above him and who very much are a power and authority, he senses that there is an engine: the love that his parents have for him. He thus must respond with a response of love. This trust, which the German personalists, in particular Gustav Siewerth, brought to light is actually fundamental. This author speaks of a "trust that makes trust," a trust that arouses trust in return. It is even the heart of his metaphysics of childhood.

Therefore, there is no faith without trust. In Christian faith, trust is that beautiful, innocent, childlike but not childish form of he who knows that he can have trust in Providence. The man who drops to his knees, who lowers himself like a child, will speak to God and implore Him, knowing that God hears him, that God is good and will give him what is best for him. He knows that God is worthy of love and worthy of trust. When you have trust in God, this gives rise to expressions of faith that are the trademark of the greatest saints! The invocation *confido tibi,* "I trust in you," addresses itself in a privileged way to the Heart of Christ, which we know contains not the slightest malice. In saying this, we speak to Christ, saying to Him, "I know that there is such love in Your Heart, and so much good, that I cannot lack in receiving from You all possible good, for I trust in You." Faith is connected to trust, and trust gives faith its humanity, its smile, and beauty.

The word engagement *brings to mind for many a world that is sentimental, or an old-fashioned concept that belongs to the past. Could you deconstruct this a priori by following the recommendations of Benedict XVI:*

> *We must strive to integrate the two [the Church and modern thought], insofar as they are compatible with each other. Being Christian must not become a sort of archaic stratum to which I cling somehow and on which I live to a certain extent alongside of modernity. Christianity is itself something living, something modern, which thoroughly shapes and forms all of my modernity—and in this sense actually embraces it.*[11]

J.L. Engagement should be seen as a privileged time. One speaks of preparation for the sacrament of marriage. Engagement conveys something more. Through a particular moment—generally at the end of a Eucharistic celebration—Christian

---

11 Pope Benedict XVI, *Light of the World,* p. 56.

fiancés declare their wish to prepare themselves: It is a promise. But it is a promise that does not build de facto—as marriage does—a community of life and love. On the other hand, each promises to the other, preserving his heart for the months of preparation to come, to give himself to her and vice versa as husband or wife. To the degree that it is a semipublic act, at the moment of a family reunion, people who love and who know the fiancés are invited to consider the fact that their hearts are from that point inhabited by this precise person with whom they foresee a project together for life. This will be marriage.

It is a privileged time because there are very deep exchanges where the fiancés express their love to each other, through words, through acts of kindness, through waiting together, through what each knows from then on about the other's feelings and what he reveals of his own. Engagement renders the time of marriage preparation richer to the extent that it already rests upon a promise. During this time when young people are about to unite their lives together in the sacrament of marriage, they seem to tell one another: "My heart already is yours, and I am preserving it for you. My thoughts and my emotions are for you." Thus there is a preparation, not only at the affective level, but also of a spiritual nature, for a promise binds. It is not a contract but rather a commitment to do everything to arrive at this moment they are waiting for. It is a time of trial because each person awaits this encounter of marriage, this expression of love in all of its affective and physical fullness. It also is a privileged time in the sense that each does not yet have the responsibility of the common life; the whole time is available to know each other better, to share in a mutual exchange, to envisage the future better . . . a time of both reciprocal cognizance and discretion. Engagement also is a kind of deliverance: Each person displays a certain weight of solitude and also is freed from it. Each person takes on his state of promise. In Italian, the fiancés are the "promised spouses"; moreover, I *Promessi Sposi* is the title of a major novel by Manzoni. The fiancés are those who are promised to become spouses, those to whom life has promised that they will become spouses.

I believe that one must not be disturbed by the fact that it is possible to backpedal. As engagement is a time of discernment, it also is a period of trial that opens up, a time of real confrontation. It is not rare for serious fiancés to decide to prolong the time of their engagement because they do not consider themselves ready. It is a privileged time because there is a great interior freedom: The fiancés discover themselves interiorly, but without giving themselves in their entire person. In particular, in true engagement, they do not give over their body. Engagement is the reciprocal gift of their two wills; this path in common for them is offered in order the better to know each other, to pray together, and to reflect together as one. It is, therefore, an experience of true fidelity, a time that educates them in guarding their heart. "My heart is promised to you! I have no future without you. You belong to my future." It is not a time where a person does whatever he wants—to the contrary! The fiancés are happy to have a unique object of love, a unique recipient of their thoughts, their affections, and their plans. Engagement is an education in the freedom of the gift.

During engagement as we have known it, and which still exists, there often is a certain gesture of a man giving a ring to his fiancée. This is not a covenant. The ring is a pledge of promise. It means: "You are the future of my life, you belong to my freedom." Engagement will become the time of discovering the freedom of the other.

This time is also without doubt marked by a certain impatience: the awaiting of the beloved. Love nourishes itself in

waiting. Man is a being of desire. During engagement, there also
is a unique spiritual opportunity: The heart that loves—and
that has made a deliberate choice for purity all the way down to
its basic demands, in looks, thought, and gestures of affection—
builds itself in the virtue of chastity. I have known couples who
live this and who remember the time of engagement as one of
tremendous spirituality.

Even if the storylines are very different.

J.L. Yes, but within our perspective of preparing for a true
Christian marriage, that is to say, of putting God at the heart of
the conjugal life that awaits the fiancés, the time of engagement
is one of immense freedom. It matters that it not be disturbed
by impurity, lack of respect, prudishness, or superficiality, for
engagement lived out in a Christian manner reveals to the fiancés the presence of God who looks over them and loves them
together, as fiancés. It is a spiritual time. Sometimes Christian
fiancés profit from it by making a retreat, a pilgrimage, or a trip
together. When this happens in a spirit of amazing discovery
of the other, the heart truly prepares itself for the celebration of
marriage. He who has promised himself sincerely to the beloved
inspires trust. He builds himself up in the responsibility of someone who has promised. To paraphrase Saint Paul, engagement is
a loss of balance "forward." One is "tended toward," as a Christian who always tends toward God and is never at equilibrium.

*How does one hold during engagement to both the physical
expression of love and respect for the other?*

J.L. Tenderness of course expresses itself also through gestures, but it is a tenderness that decides to remain chaste. It is

totally different from cohabitation. Chaste tenderness is the affective and spiritual nearness of one person to the other, but each reserves himself for the right moment, for him, for her.

Alain Quilici, who accompanied many fiancés, insists upon the great temptation "not to bear absence, to want to seize the situation in order to be the only masters of it, to make an end to this part of the mystery that is written in their adventure as fiancés, to want to demand that the other hand himself over immediately and totally, just as the People of God demand to have their own god, one that is tangible and without mystery.[12] One thinks at the same time of Genesis and original sin, which is written into the history of each couple, as well as the idolatry expressed by the event of the golden calf. What does this feeling of omnipotence suggest to you within love?

J.L. It's the confusion between the object of promise and the object of gift. The fact of being married gives you a "right" over the body of the other, an exclusivity in the loving relations. The time of engagement is one of promise, so to preempt the gift of marriage during the moment of engagement is truly to grasp at a good that is promised. Let's use a simple analogy: When a gift is promised to us, we wait with a joyous impatience. But if we take it for ourselves? Joy does not follow such an action because we no longer have anything for which to wait. What we have appropriated for ourselves is no longer offered to us! We have taken: It's the inveiglement of a free gift. To seize a gift is to deprive oneself of the joy of receiving it. There is thus a kind of bad power that acts, which in reality is a form of impotence. He who does not wait deprives himself of the joy that would be his if only he had waited.

---

12 Alain Quilici, op. cit., p. 81.

Today, one encounters far fewer persons who get engaged with all of the demands of promise and respect for the other and the other's mystery. It is a great thing to love one's future spouse and to know that one cannot know the other completely. At the same time, what a joy there is to have been able to do it, to have preserved oneself! Thus engagement becomes a time of grace: a time during which one respects the promise that life gives us. If we were to grasp this time for ourselves in an individualistic way and in a preemptive manner, there would doubtless be gratifications; but the time that precedes marriage would not have the same quality.

In order to live out the right kind of engagement, we must believe in it. That's the entire problem. In order to believe in it, we must have heard about it. In order to have heard about it, people would have had to have the courage to speak of it. These people include educators, priests, guides who accompany couples, parents. Engagement is such a precious time that one must know how to be worthy of it. Thus one doesn't cohabit or share the same accommodation, one avoids dangerous promiscuity, and one does not take a trip and share the same room. An elementary level of prudence is necessary.

Those people who are fortunate to live it are not strange fools. I am able to give you testimony from my priesthood. In several cases, I had the opportunity to accompany people who wanted to get married and who were cohabiting. During the preparation time for marriage, a level of trust was able to be established to the point that it was possible to bring up this question without difficulty. I tried to tell them, "You will get married to each other in four months. You have had all the experiences you wanted, except one: Why wouldn't you live out this experience of waiting for each other, of clothing the heart, of rediscovering one another through waiting? What is preventing you from doing so, during these four months that remain, to prepare for this ceremony, for the sacrament for which you are asking, for Christ's coming to meet you? It is not too late." I do not say that this has worked every time, but on several occasions the people considered this dimension that they were ignoring; it sometimes had a positive effect. Some people told me that they had lived as brother and sister during the months preceding their marriage and were very happy during this time: They rediscovered themselves. After having cohabited, one of these men said to me: "It is wonderful when I think that she will become my wife!" This described that which was the beginning of a spiritual journey for him, and it certainly had a profound and edifying impact upon me. You will never hear two people who cohabit say such a thing.

Moreover, we have to ask the question of how to prepare fiancés for the religious marriage ceremony often celebrated during the Mass. There are demands of dignity as well when someone wants to prepare himself for a sacrament. Two people who fundamentally have ruled out any distancing of themselves from each other over the course of the several weeks preceding their religious marriage would not fail to call into question the authenticity of their call to marriage. It is not being puritanical to raise questions in this respect. On the other hand, there is always the possibility of making the radical choice for love and thus for its demands of purity. It is not an old-fashioned idea. It matters little that cultural practice may have changed. A true culture preserves human and spiritual Christian standards as they always have existed. There is no difference within the Christian culture: Today, in 2011, it is still relevant to prepare one's heart for the extraordinary encounter of being loved, alongside the person with whom he will unite his life in Christ. It is not banal at all! It must be understood, but in order to understand it, one must have heard it from the mouth of people who believe in it. I don't see why I wouldn't tell this to people who want to get married but who are living together.

Are there countries where this might be more easily heard?

J.L. In geographical terms, there is great disparity from one culture to the next. For example, cohabitation exists very little in India, and it is the type of engagement we have described that predominates. This trend changes a little bit in the great metropolises. However, within the Christian milieu, Christians prepare themselves for marriage in the manner that Christians in our part of the world always prepared themselves, when they have an elevated idea of the mystery that they are called to live.

The true question is the following: What is our regard for Christian life? This is a fundamental question, and it applies to a young person, an elderly person, a child, a married person, a bishop, a priest . . . If I have high regard for this life of Christ in me, then its demands are connected to this intimacy with Christ. It is no longer a moral weight on my frail shoulders! Non-cohabitation is not in the first place a moral demand, but rather a demand of love. That's a completely different thing altogether. Obviously, there is a heightened morality, for love raises up all of the ethical and spiritual powers of the person.

One must not lower the bar in order for the discussion to proceed better . . .

J.L. No, of course not! Speaking from experience, some people are sensitive to what we have just said, which means that this subject is worth bringing up, being heard and developed. We are not at all judging people, we are not making moral theory, we are not writing a treatise on conjugal and family ethics. We are speaking rather of this extraordinary event that becomes like an advent of Christ in our lives, who can only strengthen our abilities to love. This then transfigures all of our actions, our choices, our decisions, and all of our behavior.

Could you speak of engagement partly as a companionship in friendship? What role does friendship play, from the moment of engagement, within the great adventure of love?

J.L. This is a good question, but reality does not rest in these terms or categories. Within this period of engagement, love chooses only to express itself through a tenderness that abstains from the sexual union that is proper to conjugal relationship. In this sense, it is not a friendship to which a person would add a love proper to spouses in a second instance, as if friendship were capable of being raised to love, and as though love integrated friendship while adding something to its physical expression. Throughout marriage, one has a love that is complete, with a singular bodily expression, that is, the sexual union of the spouses. But one has just as complete a love during engagement: a love that rightly chooses not to express itself by the totality of gestures proper to the profound union of spouses.

All love is a friendship of dilection. However, in the common meaning as people understand it, one cannot say that conjugal love is a friendship to which something would be tagged on. The time of engagement is one of authentic love, all the more authentic because one takes hold of the means to preserve it as such.

A love in potency, to take up a metaphysical category?

J.L. A love already in act, present and real, but which will receive its fruit from the moment God consecrates it through the sacrament of marriage. Then, certainly, Christian marriage is something very great indeed insofar as one reserves it for the beloved, who is received as a gift from God.

THREE

Divine Love and Human Love: Faith and Fidelity

May the God of peace Himself sanctify you wholly; and may your spirit and soul and body be kept sound and blameless at the coming of our Lord Jesus Christ. He who calls you is faithful, and He will do it.

(1 THESS. 5:23–24)

Pierre and Véronique Sanchez: *Benedict XVI summarizes in a few words the Christian understanding of marriage and the family:*

Marriage and the family are not in fact a chance sociological construction, the product of particular historical and financial situations. On the other hand, the question of the right relationship between the man and the woman is rooted in the essential core of the human being and it is only by starting from here that its response can be found. In other words, it cannot be separated from the ancient but ever new human question: Who am I? What is a human being? And this question, in turn, cannot be separated from the question about God: Does God exist?

Who is God? What is His face truly like? The Bible's answer to
these two questions unites them, and makes one a consequence
of the other: the human being is created in the image of God,
and God Himself is love. It is therefore the vocation to love that
makes the human person an authentic image of God: Man and
woman come to resemble God to the extent that they become
loving people.[13]

Is there a point in this presentation upon which you would like
to elaborate?

Bishop Jean Laffitte: Each human being who undergoes
an authentic experience of love—of true love—necessarily is
brought to know something of the divine, something of the love
of God. When God loves, He gives Himself. The essence of love
is the gift of self. God gives Himself, and He gives something of
His divine life: His life of grace, the gift of His Spirit who is the
Spirit of Love, the gift of His Heart, if you will. The man who
loves participates in this love that God gives him. When the
human being loves in turn, loving his wife or her husband, then
one expresses something of God in oneself. Authentic love—
disinterested, true, and self-giving love—has a beauty that inspires the majority of artists across all cultures. Why is the love
of a man for a woman, or of a woman for a man—and love in
other forms, such as the love of compassion, the love of children, the love of the poor—why is love the subject that is the
most represented, sung, and admired across all societies and in
all cultures? Very simply, because love transfigures. When someone loves, his face lights up. He is indwelt by a light. The gaze of

---

13 Address of His Holiness Benedict XVI to the Participants in the Ecclesial Dioc-
esan Convention of Rome, Basilica of Saint John Lateran, June 6, 2005.

one who loves is luminous. There is a joy that can be seen in the person's eyes. Something of the interior shines through, exactly as the face of Moses radiated the presence of God, whom he had seen face to face. Upon leaving the Tent of Meeting, he couldn't but allow it to shine through his face that he had encountered God. Of course, for Moses, this had to do with the brilliance of the Divine Majesty, but this brightness expressed God's love for His people and His servant.

Love illuminates, shines, and broadens the expression of the face in particular. We know that a gaze expresses the interiority of a person. A person indwelt by love is called to communicate it because love diffuses itself naturally. The notion of a love that is individual, solitary, unhappy, or does not know reciprocity, is a construction of novelists that incidentally is called romantic love, and it is often an illusion. Already in his *Treatise on Friendship*, Aristotle speaks of the reciprocity of love. Saint Thomas Aquinas developed this idea at length. Closer to our time, John Paul II spoke of reciprocity as the truthful integration of love: the fullest love, received from God and, sadly, so feebly returned by men. In relationships between people, love given and received always conveys something of God, of this familiarity and of this kinship that exists between man and God. Man is created in the image of God, not only because he is capable of intelligence and will. He also is capable of desiring the good, like God, since God is Goodness and transmits it; the Fathers of the Church fully developed these points. The human creature above all is a person who loves. When one person says to another from the bottom of his heart: "I love you, I make a covenant with you," then he expresses within his own limits what God has done with each human being. God loves each person profoundly and totally, as He has given Himself to man not only by taking on the human condition, but by giving His life within this humanity.

There is an intrinsic bond of profound kinship, of spiritual kinship and of man's dependence on God: Man loves as God loves. It is unthinkable to say, "I am going to love you for ten years . . . I will love you until the age of fifty," simply because it is impossible not to think of eternity when one loves. Love is divine in its origin: *Deus Caritas Est*. All love has a divine origin, because it is God who has taught us what love is. He loved first, and He loved so much that He created, and then saved, the nature that He had created, and that man had damaged by distancing himself from Him.

Let's come back then to Creation: "God created man in His own image, in the image of God He created him, male and female He created them" (Gen. 1:27). Not only atheists and people who are indifferent in religious matters, but even Christians too perhaps would be astonished if one were to tell them that it is not man or woman who is in the image of God, but indeed the couple formed by one and the other sex, which is to say immediately that the identity of the human being resides in love and in relation, all of which reveals to us in another manner the mystery of the Trinity. This love will be able to express itself in a conjugal manner or in the religious gift of self. That is to say, the couple is called to become a single person. How does this commitment take shape along a path where someone is called to form one single person, one flesh, or one entity with one whom he loves?

J.L. Certainly, John Paul II very much emphasized the fact that man is not a child of God only at the precise moment when Adam is created in the image of a unique God. He also expresses his identity as a child of God to the degree that he is the image of a Communion of Persons. A mark is present in him, the profound imprint of the divine Communion of Persons that is God's

Being, an ineffable mystery. It is in this sense that the couple is an image of God, a communion of persons. Pope John Paul II spoke of it in the apostolic exhortation *Mulieris Dignitatem*, on the dignity of women. In Number 7, you find why the human person, who is called to communion, is created in the image of this communion of divine persons, which expresses the very Being of God: "Man and woman, created as a 'unity of the two' in their common humanity, are called to live in a communion of love, and in this way to mirror in the world the communion of love that is in God, through which the Three Persons love each other in the intimate mystery of the one divine life."

All that is said concerning the spiritual creature and his capacity to think, to wish, and to love, and which are just as many signs of the creation of man in the image of God, remains valid. It is a deepening, an opening, and a new perspective that completes all that the great tradition of the Fathers and of the Church could say about the theme of the image of God.

The second component of your question concerns the fact of constituting one single person. The formulation of the question is provocative and thus appealing. But it is incorrect insofar as two persons who unite together never form one person. They remain two subjects having freedom. This is very true even within the structure of actions that express love. If you observe the structure of the bodily dynamism of human love, of masculine and feminine sexuality, you easily notice a nuptial dialogue, but it does not obey the rules of fusion. Forming "one flesh" does not mean forming one person. In fact, the spouses unite their bodies and, in this sense, they form one flesh. However, it is only at an analogical level that one speaks of a "union of spirits" or of a "union of hearts," precisely in order to signify a communion. In playing on these words, you could say a *common union*. Why? Because we have two ontological realities that are very distinct from each other. The two spouses, even at the moment of greatest intimate union, remain two subjects in freedom. In the very unfolding of these expressions, there is always the possibility for one to hold back. There is never a real fusion. One forms "a single being" to the degree that there is a communion of desire, of feelings, and of affection, but, within the choice of love, each remains sovereign in his given freedom until the very end. One flesh does not mean forming one person, even if there is a forming of one flesh when the two bodies are profoundly united.

But being united, does that also mean for example that one tries to have as much patience for the faults of another as one would need to have for one's own? Is it necessary, like Saint Francis de Sales, to try to forbid what he called "rash judgment," which involves fitting the other into the idea one has of him, something that obviously has an impact on the quality of relations between spouses? When one lives within the intimacy of a family, do sins of thought have a profound impact on the quality of the general atmosphere?

J.L. I believe it absolutely, and it is very correct: There is neither neutrality nor indifference in thoughts. Many people imagine that to the degree they have not acted badly, they haven't faltered. Few people are conscious of the importance, and at times of the gravity, of sins of thought. Men are not infallible. No man has perfect mastery of his thoughts; the spirit can allow itself to be captivated by bad suggestions and reckless judgments. It is reasonable to be sufficiently aware of it. It is true that rash judgments wound, eat away at, and impede the communication of grace, as well as the communication between persons, simply put. Rash judgments give birth to suspicions, doubts, wariness of the other, and various movements of which we need to be watchful. How? By keeping the memory of God in our heart and thoughts. Saint Augustine called this *recordatio*, or literally, "memory of the heart." Prayer helps in this domain. It is impossible always to keep guard over an evenness of tone, mood, and thought, especially when our spirit and heart are not indwelt by the thought of God. The Christian must be very convinced of this. One speaks here of the reality and the seriousness of the Christian life at the highest level of its demands. It does not suffice merely not to commit acts contrary to the law of God; rather, one is required to perform actions that have a spiritual and supernatural expressiveness, texture, and depth—for example, to see the beauty and uniqueness of the other. You sometimes have people who love each other, and nevertheless, each one doesn't stop speaking badly of the family of the other! But how can we forget that the family of the other is his or hers, to which the other person is united in heart, in love, and in affection? One can wound the other by brooding over the defects of the other person's mother, father, and family traditions. It is important to be prudent, and it is equally a question of sensitivity. Love has a correct expression, a life that refines the emotions of the heart at the same time as the moral conscience. Sensitivity is the exquisite perfume of love. I'll give you another example: Look at the quality of the loving relationship between Jacques and Raïssa Maritain. Read their letters, exchanged after forty years of marriage. They constantly lived paying the utmost attention to each other's expectations and desires, also with this deliberate choice that they shared in common, to serve and to love God first. We must revisit frequently the examples of couples

who were saints. Between Luigi and Maria Beltrame Quattrocchi, who were the first beatified couple, hundreds of letters were exchanged that now are published. These letters
express, just as with the Maritains, a quality of relationship that shines through each of them. And what finally do
we say of the parents of Saint Thérèse, the Blesseds Louis
and Zélie Martin? There again, read the letters that they
wrote to each other. Look at the watch case designed and
created by Louis for his wife. Within these couples, and in
thousands of unknown others, everything is done out of joy
for the other, to be a servant of the other's joy. There is
no place there for rash judgments, for doubt, suspicion, or
jealousy. On the contrary, one finds utmost respect for the
freedom of the other. It is the miracle of love. A person who
is truly beloved feels more and more free to act, to work, to
have an activity. It is just like the trust of which we spoke
between parents and children.

The Song of Solomon confirms that nuptial language is the most
adapted for permitting God to express His love for His people:

I slept, but my heart was awake.
Hark! my beloved is knocking.
"Open to me, my sister, my love,
my dove, my perfect one;
for my head is wet with dew,
my locks with the drops of the night."

(Song of Sol. 5:2)

Rarely has a text joined together so high a mysticism with so deli-
cate a sensuality. Christian Puritanism without a doubt had to pay

an additional price, levied by May 1968.[14] *But since Vatican II, the Magisterium—and we are thinking in particular of the teaching of John Paul II—made huge advances in the understanding of sexuality and conjugality. Could you give us some examples?*

J.L. Up until roughly a century ago, marriage was considered above all as a social act. One thought of it in terms of its objective value, its divine origin, the demands of its human institution, and its objective truth and beauty. But one did not linger on the intentions and emotions of the two contracting persons. One didn't enter yet into the subjectivity of the spouses, into their interiority. The beginning of the twentieth century was when philosophy, anthropology, and the human sciences worked out, deepened, and clarified to an enormous extent an entire sphere in the knowledge of man, in particular the dimension of his interiority and his judgment—in brief, every way that a subject wants, desires, and thinks. Within the perspective of service of the person, we alluded at the beginning of our conversation to the personalist currents that were devoted to studying moral phenomena, for example Edith Stein for empathy, Dietrich von Hildebrand for the essence of love, or Gabriel Marcel for the mystery of the family. During this period, personalist philosophy certainly contributed to placing value on the riches of the knowledge of human interiority. We find traces of this in several documents of the Magisterium of the Church. I think here of Pius XI's encyclical on the sacrament of marriage, *Casti Connubii*, in 1930. In this text, Pius XI said for example that

---

14 In May 1968, France was rocked by student protests that spread to the general population; the protests caused a major political crisis and liberalized social attitudes in the area of sexuality.

each of the spouses is a minister for the sanctification of the other. Much later, the radio broadcasts and addresses of Pope Pius XII to fiancés accentuated this perspective. You also know the texts that afterward inspired a true spiritual theology of marriage, such as Numbers 48 through 52 of the Pastoral Constitution *Gaudium et Spes* of the Second Vatican Council, the apostolic exhortation *Familiaris Consortio* in 1981, and the *Letter to Families*. Marriage is seen not only in terms of its essence, but also in the dynamism that encompasses the persons. It does not suffice to say that marriage is holy because it was created by God. That is true, and we must say it because it is fundamental. However, we must also say that spouses sanctify each other in marriage. They are called to holiness, and they sanctify one another in all of their communal life. Obviously, we should also mention *Humanae Vitae* of Pope Paul VI. When Paul VI studies the object of the conjugal act, he indicates that this love perfects the spouses as long as they respect the nature of the act, the two unitive and procreative dimensions of which cannot be separated deliberately. He thus expressed the characteristics of conjugal love: a love fully human, total, faithful and exclusive, and fruitful.

From the beginning of the pontificate of John Paul II, the impressive series of catecheses on human love commences. They form a true cathedral, an ensemble of 133 catecheses where the mystery of love and marriage is approached from a Biblical, philosophical, anthropological, spiritual, sacramental, and ethical perspective. Nothing is missing in this approach. Never before had anyone written—to my knowledge even in secular literature—a study so vast on human love in all of its components. It should not surprise us that critical editions exist in at least ten languages, and that the thought that unfolds in them does not cease to bear fruit throughout the entire world. And how could we fail to mention the 1986 instruction *Donum Vitae*, which concerns the transmission of life? In this text, Pope John Paul II speaks about acts that lead to human procreation, which must be truly loving. A negative judgment is made concerning the acts of artificial procreation, to the degree that they separate human life from its concrete bond with the profound union between a man and a woman.

In all of these texts, the concern of the Church is to show humanity what human sexuality is: The gift of life is bound to an act of love. To insist upon this point is a new thing. A century ago, one spoke of human life as a gift of God, which it in fact is, a sacred gift, but its immediate connection with the act that expresses the love of the spouses was not demonstrated. It is an absolute novelty, a Copernican revolution within the Magisterial expression of human love and the promotion and defense of human life. You will notice that the texts on the family delivered by Benedict XVI since the beginning of his pontificate continue along this line of thought. The first chapter of *Deus Caritas Est* is an exploration of the divine love that unites *eros* and *agapé* with great finesse. To speak of *divine eros* is revolutionary in its expression.

The mystery that is contemplated here sees men as associated with divine will and action. We are only just beginning to see the fruits of this entire undertaking. One of these fruits is the John Paul II Institute, which studies marriage and family and is present across five continents, and also all of the catecheses of John Paul II.

Did John Paul II in fact write the catecheses?

J.L. He wrote them out down to the last comma. I can tell you that the next-to-last critical edition was carried out in the

English language by Michael Waldstein, an Austrian professor who now teaches in the United States. He took up again the titles and subtitles of the Polish manuscript that he had received authorization to consult. The first critical edition of these catecheses in the Italian language was accomplished by the John Paul II Institute in Rome in 1986. And now we already have arrived at the eighteenth edition! It is true that the majority of these texts, written by John Paul II himself, have their origin in the work of the philosopher Karol Wojtyła, since his major work on this subject, *Love and Responsibility*, was published in 1960, eighteen years before he became Pope.

This demonstrates that the Church evolves and progresses . . .

J.L. The Church evolves in the expression of a mystery that she does not cease to contemplate. However, she transmits the same truth at the service of the same mystery, demonstrating its richness to an ever greater degree through progressive illuminations. But she expresses the same mystery. There is no substantial novelty in terms of what Christ did when He raised the union of spouses to the dignity of a sacrament. The Church studies, deepens, and utilizes all of the sciences while preserving the same intention to teach what John Paul II called "God's design for marriage and the family" when he was speaking of the "*consilium Dei matrimonii ac familiae.*" The Church is always at the service of God's design, but she enters ever more profoundly into this service. When you contemplate and meditate upon the good given by God, you discover more and more the treasures, the nuances, the facets, and the colors that are unveiled there little by little. The Church benefits in this from the culture in which she finds herself. She benefits from the contribution of German and French personalist philosophy, as we have said, just as she once benefitted from Roman law. She will benefit from other contributions in the future.

The recommendations of the Church in matters of sexuality are the subject of constant misunderstanding on the part of the French public in particular, by virtue of a vivacious Gallicanism that the media develop and accentuate as they please. Opinion comes to a halt at the surface level of the question, without striving to understand the reasons behind the Catholic requirements. Benedict XVI even speaks in very clear language, but the media seem to take malevolent pleasure in orchestrating a general deafness:

> *If we separate sexuality and fecundity from each other in principle, which is what the use of the pill does, then sexuality becomes arbitrary. Logically, every form of sexuality is of equal value. This approach to fecundity as something apart from sexuality, so far apart that we may even try to produce children rationally and no longer see them as a natural gift, was, after all, quickly followed by the ascription of equal value to homosexuality.[15]*

What do you have to say concerning this subject?

J.L. In your severe but realistic assessment, there are two components. One element is *ad intra*: when you speak of Gallicanism, which refers to an ecclesial current of thought proper to our country. It has historical roots and developed out of wanting a certain distance in relation to Rome, which was considered to be intrusive or centralizing. Unfortunately, Gallicanism is only the French expression of a reality that is not an exclusive

---

15 Pope Benedict XVI, *Light of the World*, p. 146.

prerogative of the French context. At home [in my country], this issue concerns an ecclesial sensibility that certainly has not disappeared, but which without a doubt makes itself felt less than in the past. Moreover, one comes across other questions and problems that we encounter less [in our French culture]. Every culture has a weakness with regard to the assimilation and integration of the Church's truths. We are not exaggerating what is real and well known, but we cannot generalize to all spiritual families and to all persons. What inspires the dynamic of the Church—the very expression of ecclesial communion—does so according to different conditions, depending on the culture or country.

On the other hand, the *ad extra* dimension that your question evokes relates to the influence of a vision and a culture imposed by the media. There is a real difficulty due to the global nature of this diffusion of cultural models that trivialize the practice of sexuality. Less and less sensitive to the beauty of sacrificial love, such models express the notion of a sexuality exclusively founded upon personal gratification and the search for maximum pleasure. The reality of this widespread hedonism requires us to be firm in the defense of Christian and human values concerning love and marriage. We can try to do so without tension or a paranoid view of society, but also without naïveté. This scenario brings to mind a series of questions on the education of young people, children, adolescents, and families. It is a great challenge that must be addressed with confidence and also with great determination. Witness to love demands steadfastness and courage.

In spite of the violence directed at her, the Church nevertheless is not content with dictating theoretical norms. She proposes, among other things, to be a help to persons affected by AIDS, which is one of the great contemporary wounds of love: "The Church does more than anyone else, because she does not speak from the tribunal of the newspapers, but helps her brothers and sisters where they are actually suffering."[16] *Do you have any examples of this kind of concrete commitment by the Church in this area, or of other actions that allow the Church to ensure a genuine service of her authority toward the persons to whom she speaks?*

J.L. Yes. The example of AIDS is very well known, as it has been discussed much over the past several years. The issue of AIDS and its transmission has taken a polemic turn, as the positions of the Church have been challenged by preventive measures taken generally by health care workers of different countries, measures that confine themselves often to a method that is exclusively founded upon the distribution of contraceptives. Efforts of education in fidelity, self-mastery, and limiting oneself to a single partner are ignored, actions that have been very efficacious—as may be observed in several countries of East Africa. The Church is extremely active in the care of those people suffering from AIDS. In Africa, she runs more than a quarter of the institutions for the care and accompaniment of sick persons, something that people generally don't know . . . not to mention the educational institutions for children, adolescents, and young people in this domain. The outreach work done by several Christian organizations in Africa is exemplary. I think in particular of what the African Federation of Family Associations has succeeded in doing, with very little means.

AIDS is not the only health problem. There also are many other illnesses in the world that are just as serious. The first is malaria, from which millions of people die each year. Other

---

16 Pope Benedict XVI, *Light of the World*, p. 118.

sicknesses are more rare but still exist: I am thinking here of leprosy, of illnesses that fuel a considerable infant mortality rate within health care institutions that lack proper infrastructure from the point of view of hygiene.

I would like to underscore that in the countries where Christians are very much in the minority, the Church is able to serve an important role in public health. Let's take the case of India, for example: Christians represent about 4 percent of the country's population. Around 25 percent of clinics, hospitals, and dispensaries—as well as elementary, primary, and secondary teaching establishments—are animated by the Church. How can a population that represents only 4 percent of a country participate in such a manner in the common good of a gigantic nation of more than a billion inhabitants? You have here an example that is never mentioned in the media, and about which Western Catholics aren't even aware, where we get an idea of the solicitude of Christians and of Churches of various traditions in service to the poor and sick. And what do we say of the free clinics and hospitals, as well as the efforts of religious men and women in Africa? Or of the involvement in the sphere of eliminating illiteracy? In Africa, 50 percent of works to counter illiteracy are conducted by Christians . . . an enormous contribution. You have religious congregations that have consecrated their essential human resources to this humble development, outside of any polemic upheaval. And this is not known . . . In all of the cases, if this fact is known, it is kept silent.

Following up on what you have just presented, where the Church is involved and gives of herself to the service of all people, without discrimination in culture or religion, could you speak to us of the efforts of the John Paul II institutes across the world in their service to the family? These institutions of formation, of which there still is no presence in France, are little known.

J.L. The Church is involved in institutes of formation that sometimes have an unexpected fruitfulness, of which the John Paul II Institute for Studies on Marriage and Family is a good example. At its origin, the Institute was born on May 13, 1981, along with the Pontifical Council for the Family, which I have the honor of serving as its Secretary. You will remember that this date marks the assassination attempt against John Paul II, the same day as the feast of Our Lady of Fatima. On that day, in the afternoon during a public audience, the Pope was to announce the foundation of these two organizations. John Paul II desired at the time to develop an institute of studies at the university level, scientific in scope, concerning all of the questions tied to human love within the realm of fundamental and special moral ethics, the humanities, and bioethics . . . a desire realized as the Institute for Marriage and Family that later became the John Paul II Institute. He also wanted to create a new council in the Vatican that would be consecrated more particularly to the pastoral service of the family.

It is very significant, it seems to me, to see that these two organizations were founded on the day when the Church was made even more fruitful by the blood of a genuine confessor of the faith, who, what's more, would be declared Blessed on May 1, 2011. The John Paul II Institute developed first in Rome, and different countries since then have asked for the opening of a session among them. Thus the sessions of Washington, Mexico, Salvador de Bahia, Cotonou in Benin, Changanacherry in India, Melbourne in Australia, and Valencia in Spain were established, and other sections are currently in the process of being erected in South Korea, English-speaking Africa in Zambia, the

Philippines, and Lebanon. The originality of these various sections comes from a genuine unity of teaching in fundamental matters, in conjunction with autonomy in management.

The Church only founds new institutions in order to fulfill a particular need. She is free to create new structures or, eventually, to transform them or to bring them to a close. In the case of the John Paul II Institute, we have a university organization of pontifical right. For its part, the Council for the Family enjoys a considerable importance to the degree that, concerning questions on marriage and the family, it is at the service of all of the families of the world, most often through the mediation of marriage and family associations. Another example would be the Pontifical Academy for Life, which was born at the conclusion of an intense dialogue between Pope John Paul II and Jérôme Lejeune, whose cause for beatification was opened several years ago by the Archdiocese of Paris. Founded in 1994, this academy—under the impetus most notably of Elio Sgreccia—has contributed considerably to the debate on all of the questions related to the defense and promotion of human life.

One also can remark that among all of the great religions, Catholicism is alone in intervening to make known her positions through the media, knowing perfectly well that she exposes herself to misunderstandings and acrimony. What do the Muslims think of abortion? What do the Jewish people think of homosexual marriage? One does not have the least sketch of an answer concerning these questions. Is this phenomenon due specifically to the fact that the Church throughout the world has the same leader in the person of the successor to Peter? Or could one also speak to the proper courage of the Catholic Church, who does not fear proclaiming the Good News while putting herself forward, vulnerably, among wolves?

J.L. We can't say that other religious traditions do not offer a response concerning the great problems that you mention. However, the stand they take is not always audible, due to the diversity of traditions that sometimes belong to them. The Jewish people hold positions that are known in matters of the defense of human life. There is a similar Muslim tradition. I have participated in colloquia with Muslims on questions concerning the family in Lebanon and Africa, in particular on the question of mixed marriages between Catholics and Muslims. There also exists within the other traditions an exploration of the mystery of love and the institution of marriage.

. However, it is absolutely true that the Church is the only one constantly to "intervene," which comes from a concrete and practical reality: She is the only one to have a Magisterium, for she respects her responsibility to enlighten men on what is good for them, on what will bring them happiness versus what will not make them happy, and on what goes against the natural law and divine law. She holds in this respect to her conviction and certainty, and also to her knowledge, that Christ has entrusted to her the keys of His Church, through the voice of the Apostles at first and then through their successors. She has the assurance of being aided by the Holy Spirit in her mission of transmitting Christian doctrine and of expressing what must be accepted in a definitive manner concerning matters of faith but also in morals.

Several Magisterial texts rely not only on apostolic and Magisterial tradition, but on the demands of natural law (*Humanae Vitae* and *Evangelium Vitae*, for example). The Church is the only one to exercise a Magisterium that, for the Catholic faith, is received as a clarifying authority guiding all men. The person of faith adheres to the teaching of the Church. To follow the Church only for reasons that are more or less spiritual, while being disinterested in the ethical implications of her teachings in moral matters, does not suffice. In reality, the totality of what the Church transmits, which is the responsibility of the Apostles and of their successors united to the successor of Peter, creates sincere adherence in the heart of a believer. Peter had a specific responsibility with regard to the College of Apostles.

The Church has one voice that makes itself heard. She is attacked because she is not always understood. Her work is sometimes recognized outside of her borders, especially when her word appears clearly to be prophetic concerning the events of the world. In recent history, we have seen several conflicts in which the Church was the only one to take positions, the pertinence of which have been recognized after the fact. Very often, the Church has the courage to take a position in which she knows she will be not only in the minority, but also isolated. She is driven thus to give her testimony, although it costs her. This action is part of her mission, of her very being. Finally, let us add that she has intervened several times with success in the resolution of conflicts.

The Catholic Church proposes a pedagogical idea of love: You learn to love, and you can spend all of life in this apprenticeship. This is why the family plays a key role in helping children discover the joy of growing in love. It is plausible that the modern world, especially in the West, is no longer capable of tolerating the magisterial teaching of whatever authority there may be. But it is also true that the Christian idea of love is demanding. With much discernment, Alain Quilici proposes the following reflection: "It is not so simple to be loved, especially by God, and to live at the height of this divine love."[17] Is this consent not the decisive step on the way of love, and a step that must be renewed each day?

---

17 Alain Quilici, op. cit., p. 48.

J.L. Yes, without any doubt! To adhere to Christ and to try to correspond in the best possible manner to the height of one's own vocation to love, with the demands that this implies in terms of personal conduct, is a step that needs to be renewed each day with the help of the Holy Spirit. We cannot depend solely upon our own personal strength and will. It is true that today there is growing difficulty in conceiving the legitimacy of an authority, whether it emanates from parents, institutions, or teachers. The very idea of a Magisterium disturbs, even in certain parts of the Church. The adherence of the believer to the Church's teachings renews itself each day through his concrete dependence upon the grace of God and the spiritual vitality that it confers. It is not easy to be faithful always in everything. But from day to day, God gives us the grace to do so more and more. The saints are those people who lived the present moment continually in the grace of God. Anchored in His friendship, the observance of His precepts lived well in prayer became second nature to them, a natural breathing.

Love must be renewed each day. No situation is irreparably compromised. The Church as teacher is patient and fundamentally optimistic. Are you as well?

J.L. The Church is optimistic to the degree she is conscious that she has the means of salvation received from the Lord Himself. Her reasons are thus spiritual, ecclesiological, and theological. Her evaluation of history is eschatological. The Church knows that Christ is the conqueror of death, of suffering, and of evil. This is in her nature: Fundamentally she only transmits the hope of Christ to men. She cannot be defeatist, melancholic, nostalgic, or old-fashioned. She accepts the totality of her history, as she knows that at no moment has the assistance of the

Holy Spirit failed her. The Church then integrates all of her tradition to the degree that she adheres to all that Christ has done for her, assisting her throughout the centuries. She is the bearer of hope. That having been said, she also has the means of discerning what may be a threat to man, what is a source of injustice, what threatens peace, everything that separates man from God. She is a realist. Most profoundly, however, she is turned toward God's present and not toward any kind of idealistic future. God's present embraces the future.

The Christian family finally has two great models of reference: the Holy Trinity and the Holy Family. My question concerns virginity. In the Holy Family, I observe that its three members—Joseph, Mary, and Jesus—are virgins. Could you speak to us about virginity in the bosom of the family, as one associates it more generally with the priesthood and religious life?

J.L. Your observation is correct. There is a very great affinity between the state of marriage and the state of consecrated virginity. We must take this as our starting point, as one state of life clarifies the other. First of all, consecrated virginity is not an amputation of the entire affective dimension of man and woman. It is the choice of a voluntary and coherent love, a "foolish" love, in order to take up again the expression of Jacques Maritain. It is a love of God such that one offers everything to Him. It is in its essence an act of love and not an act of restriction. We offer to God what is most profoundly from our heart and our affectivity, as a total gift of our person. It is something that is achieved daily. It is not an acquired state, for man—in the earthly condition that is his—is not an angelic creature. He must always renew this act of donation to God from all of his being.

In the state of marriage, it is well said that what's involved is an act of love that leads to the gift of the entire person to another, an act of profound and authentic love that also is a mediation of holiness, of friendship with God. Why? Because God is at the heart of this gift that each person gives to the other. Within one or the other state of life, there is the presence of God. However, in the state of marriage, there is the mediation of conjugal love. For this reason, marriage is a sacrament. On the other hand, consecrated virginity is not a sacrament. There is no sacrament of religious life. The reason for this is that consecrated virginity already anticipates what the state of the Kingdom will be. There is a prophetic and eschatological dimension within the choice of consecrated virginity. Within the state of marriage, there is also very much a supernatural goal, but the way of human love in its bodily expression is a mediation that stops at the end of human life. In fact, Saint Paul says that marriage is a reality for the life of this world. In the Kingdom, there is neither husband nor wife, nor mother nor father, the Apostle says. That is not to say that the bonds that are woven during marriage might be lost for eternity, not at all. But what subsists from this conjugal life is the authentic love of the spouses, in its fullness, a love that will be nourished by the divine source of all love. This is one of the reasons why preparation for marriage is so important. Marriage in effect is a possibility of making human love a privileged means of meeting God and of preparing oneself for eternal life without putting up obstacles against the love of God. On the other hand, choosing a human union while excluding God *a priori* is to deprive this relationship of its genuine compass. One must see that to the degree that sacramental conjugal love integrates the loving and acting presence of God and of Christ throughout life, it leads one necessarily to eternal friendship with God.

In consecrated virginity, there is no need for mediation. This is why there is no visible sign: It is the choice of a total gift that anticipates in some way the manner of living that is proper to the Kingdom of God. Our speculation does not have access to the mystery of eternal love. We know of it simply by what the glory of the Saints has made manifest to us, as well as the light with which the Resurrection of Christ illuminates our life. We know something of it also through the joy that we feel sometimes when we live even weakly some realities of the Kingdom: I think in particular of charity in its theological sense, the love of the spiritual good of the other.

I return to the notion of "person." It is the fundamental contribution of Christianity to a culture that roots itself within the revelation of the one God in three Persons. We are created in the image and likeness of God. Here is the foundation of our being: We are persons destined to enter into relation with others in order to grow in love and to come back toward our vital source, which is God. The Church presents this anthropology at the service of man as something universal. Along the lines of the Second Vatican Council, the Church places herself at the service of society. She does not work only for her parish.

J.L. The Church has the vocation to come out from herself as an institution. The movement that carries her is an authentically spiritual and divine movement, a movement of love: She is then carried beyond her limits to bear witness to the love of Christ and especially to preach, for example, the Word, service, and attention to those people who suffer from all sorts of needs. She has a very tight bond with the common good of society, a bond that is similar to that which the family has with society, and of which we already have spoken: The family is at the service of society. There is also a bond between the Church and the common good, for the Church cannot disinterest herself from the good of men, or from the good of society. Each member of the Church also is a citizen. Besides that, the Church herself is a society that bears a common good proper to her, the communion of saints.

And yet, Western society is confronted with secularization, with the loss of Christian roots from this anthropology that nevertheless has given birth to all humanistic values. However, Western society now clashes with another phenomenon that it has difficulty defining, and it's the same for the Church: I would like to speak of Islam, which places within our societies of Christian origin a model of the person that is different from the Christian model. In Islam, man is not created in the image of God, because God is not One in Three Persons. This God is so transcendent that He becomes inaccessible. What could you say about this subject, which the Church will have to confront more and more, and more explicitly?

J.L. Within Islam, there is a patrimony of traditions in the plural. There is great diversity from one tradition to another: Shiite, Sunni, and Sufi traditions ... It already is difficult to speak in a unified manner of Islam, especially as Islam does not have a magisterial code that imposes itself upon all Muslims. The intellectual traditions vary among themselves from one center to the next, from one university to another. Today, one cannot avoid speaking of Islam within Western societies. It is important, therefore, to consider the issue carefully while also noting that it is a fraught question. The reason is that we are in an evolving situation. If Islam's relationship with Western society were a stable issue, contained within its own borders, one could present some elements for discussion and expand upon them. However, even without reference to any political scene, one should admit the fact that we find ourselves in an evolving situation. In certain countries, this evolution is more accelerated. The question that arises is not so much Islam in its multiform reality, but the capacity of Western societies to be interlocutors with Islam correctly within this context of evolution. What can Western societies transmit and receive at the same time? What can a society transmit that no longer believes in itself, does not take up means for its own demographic survival, despises its cultural and historical patrimony, or disowns its historical roots?

One can reflect endlessly upon the possible exchanges with Islam. I have had the occasion of participating in several mixed meetings on the themes that we have mentioned, within a university or ecclesial context. There was no lack of subjects to discuss: the concept of marriage, mixed marriages, defense of human life and its ethical implications, and religious liberty. But your question goes well beyond what one is able to elaborate upon in a university and strictly intellectual approach. Your question is more demanding and consists of saying to oneself: "In the current configuration of our society, which continues to evolve, what is it possible to offer to all of society such that there may be a life and a living together that would be normal, within an environment that would be as peaceful as possible?" The various aspects of this question are very diverse. Some of them relate to social, economic, and financial balance, others to a purely demographic perspective, which in effect is a very serious problem in the West. The question of the relation with Islam raises questions from its different angles concerning the decisions of political officials.

An immediate avenue that could be taken would be a common effort with Muslims in areas concerning some decisive issues confronting society: respect for human life, the conditions of family life, understanding better the concrete implications of new bioethical laws, the protection of children and young people, the issue of invading the intimacy of persons through technologies, and the morality of the public sphere. All of these domains interest Christians as much as Muslims. One also may add the permeable character of our society: We have abolished distances, and we have abolished time. Informed in real time of everything that happens on the surface of the planet, one forgets that time and space are two great anthropological structures that until now have given foundation to the life of men. These structures have been as if abolished by the entrance of technology into people's interiority. During the course of his recent visit to Venice, Pope Benedict XVI used a curious term, taken from a contemporary sociologist, to define the fragility of our societies that are both permeable and unstable: He called them "liquid" societies. The term *liquid* applied to a society expresses its fluidity, its precarious stability, its changing, relative, and ephemeral character, and its inconsistency.

You mention time and space. Is it also a matter of relation with history that is involved today?

J.L. The reading of the history of our own country by children and adolescents leaves you speechless: The teaching of history in France is practically limited to the last century, to the last half-century. Only thirty years ago, one began with the French Revolution. The young people of today often have not set aside one hour of their lives to consider the history of their country before 1789 or before 1914. It is an anthropological reality. When you have a history that stretches across two millennia, you cannot amputate eighteen or nineteen twentieths from these two millennia. If you do so, you are no longer the bearer of this wealth. You will not integrate what, on the other hand, your fathers integrated: currents intermingled in time, with slowness.

I would like to make two brief statements on the demographic question. Simple projections that are reasonable and reliable demonstrate that our traditional societies have become extraordinarily unstable. We are at the threshold of a very great evolution that renders it impossible to foresee the manner in which the social bond will be safeguarded. The conditions of this safeguarding are the direct responsibility of governing officials. Christians, for their part, can only dialogue truthfully and without fear inasmuch as they live their faith, when they are conscious of their own identity and take it up without shyness. We find ourselves on ground that becomes eminently political, where positions taken are often short-term and affected by prejudices, choices, and ideologies. Once again: In order serenely to tackle this question, we must ask the question concerning our own riches and our own identity. Then, we ask the question concerning the other. This is the path of the Christian and the way of love: What do I have to offer? In the society where I live, and which I did not choose, within these diverse currents that I cannot refuse through violence, what can I give? I am confronted by my limitations but also by that of which I am the bearer. Behind this, the love of the common good and of one's country, its history, and its traditions is at stake.

I recently read the title of an article that basically raised in substance this question: Can Islam be absorbed into our societies? Our Western societies are Christian, saturated by Christianity, even if they have rejected it or do not declare it. The Muslim family does not function at all upon the same foundations. Could there be two models of the family within the same society?

J.L. You insist very much upon Islam, which demonstrates the consistency of this question. Western tradition, marked by Christianity, has always defended a legislative model founded upon monogamy and monandry, and thus upon a family cell founded on the bond between two parents. I remind you in passing that our society is beginning to distance itself from these models that have constituted it throughout the ages. In the Muslim tradition, there is a real preference among numerous Muslims—intellectuals and religious alike—for monogamy. All the same, there is within the common understanding of Islam this idea of four possible spouses, an idea implying a family model that does not rest necessarily upon monogamous marriage.

Once again, I am sorry to say it in a manner that perhaps is not politically correct: If we belong to a society that calls into question its own secular idea of marriage that is not only monogamous but also heterosexual and open to welcoming children, then it must not astonish us that this society feels itself helpless with respect to the rise of a tradition where the concern for a monogamous family is not first in importance. If you do not defend the genuine nature of the conjugal institution at the legislative level, you can no longer respectfully confront other traditions. The problem, in fact, is ours. If we say, for example: Let us establish homosexual "marriage" equal to existing heterosexual marriage, we may legislate, but we will do so regardless of the fact that there is no more ethical justification for homosexual marriage than there is for marriage within the context of polygamy.

If we have a discordant dialogue with Islam, it is because Western society no longer has anything to offer as a credible social model. For Muslims, having four wives is not something that's permitted but rather a juridical institution. In the same manner, polygamy in Africa obeys juridical codes that manifest at times much more respect toward the third or fourth spouse than a Western Don Juan does toward his or her partner! The problem, therefore, is not to abdicate what has built us up. It is impossible to approach these delicate questions with a sort of ideal that is rather vague and consensual—and which in reality keeps Muslims from being Muslims and Christians from being Christians—and to recognize that it is within a Christian matrix that our European societies have been formed throughout the centuries.

The Church respects the freedom of conscience of each person. It is a contribution of the Second Vatican Council. It equally is one of the foundations of Western democracy. But what comes of it in the case of mixed marriages? During marriage preparation, does one ask the Muslim party to accept and to recognize this principle of freedom of conscience—or freedom of worship?

J.L. When you say "freedom of conscience," that brings to mind two things: that which you presented in your question; but for some years now, *freedom of conscience* also refers to ethical choices, notably with all that is developing surrounding the debate on conscientious objection in ethical and bioethical issues. The latter meaning has already been mentioned, and we must distinguish between the two. Your question refers to the inviolable character of a human conscience that must be able freely to render to God the worship that is due Him. This tradition has always existed within the Church, and it has nothing to do with religious relativism.

In the case of mixed marriages, I will say that the first question that arises apropos a Christian person who is Catholic, who desires to marry and who is sufficiently believing in terms of practicing his own religion, is the following: Is this person completely enlightened concerning the manner in which he will be called to live and to practice his faith in the future, and to transmit it to his children? The problem lies there. I am not saying that mixed marriages are to be prohibited, but simply that someone who desires to contract a marriage should ask these real questions beforehand.

Does the Church help such a person?

J.L. The Church helps him if she offers him the opportunity to prepare himself seriously for marriage. Often, the only contact such people have with the Church is a request for dispensation due to disparity of cult. In reality, who is requesting the dispensation? Is it a Christian person, a simple nonpracticing Christian, or a person who has faith and puts it into practice? In each case, it's good if this is clarified. We can imagine that at the moment when one person requests a document of dispensation, a discussion can be held—also with the Muslim party—such that each person may be clear as to the consequences. The entire question of mixed marriages is very complex. There is a necessity, a duty to inform.

So, the first questions to be asked by the Catholic party: "What am I willing to do with the faith received at my baptism? I am engaged in an affective relationship and would like to unite my life with a man or a woman I love. How will I articulate this choice with my faith? Does my faith exist? Is it destined to continue to exist?" If I do not ask myself these questions, I do not address the problem. There is a response that can be given only by the subject of these personal choices. I am persuaded that if the majority of Catholic persons were enlightened, they often would renounce what will be a very great difficulty for them, at least for those who still value the faith of their baptism.

A connected question to bring this part to a close: Many marriages end in divorce. Persons who prepare the engaged can often see that couples are not ready. In agreeing to marry them, should they not rather warn them to put their wedding off rather than leaving them imprisoned within a marriage that is doomed to failure?

J.L. When the priest is convinced in conscience that the marriage about to be celebrated will be null for reasons connected to precise facts, obviously he must not celebrate the marriage. When he has grave doubts, and when he cannot oppose this marriage because these doubts are not totally convincing, it is appropriate that he express his doubts and write a "letter of reservation" that will be preserved in the marriage file, and he celebrates the marriage as best as possible. But well beyond these specific, canonical aspects, it is suitable for the spouses to receive a preparation appropriate to them. In this preparation, the contact that the pastor has with each of the future spouses is essential, as it is in such personal relationships that things can emerge.

As for the difficulty that you call to mind, the dissolution of marriage by divorce is a wound that touches a great number of couples in our societies, in certain regions up to one out of two marriages. Certainly, one cannot dissuade fiancés from getting married under the pretext that statistically there is a higher proportion of marriages that end up in divorce! It is contrary to hope and also contrary to respect for the freedom of persons who themselves each have the means to overcome obstacles, as well as not to divorce, in order to stay united. At the spiritual level, one of these means is a Christian life that is consistent and coherent with the sacrament requested. It is not at all normal for people to get married in the Church and then the next day no longer to step into the Church, inaugurating instead forty years of pagan life. When a serious problem arises, they no longer ask the Church to help them, since they never asked the Church to give them the means of salvation, or the means for eternal life and a life of grace. There is a coherence of the Christian life with married life, which one prepares to take on.

The second point is that in the life of men, there have to be human, anthropological rites. When people live in society, *a fortiori* [all the more strongly] within the close society that is marriage, it is necessary that there be a practice of reconciliation and of the forgiveness of offenses, including light ones; that there be a culture of peace, concord, and communion. The people and youth who have never learned to ask for forgiveness will never be disposed to pardon each other. When a difficulty arises, it will be easiest to go completely overboard. Forgiveness is central in the preparation for marriage. Personally, I have never conducted marriage preparation without consecrating a meeting to pardon, to reconciliation, and to the demands that they involve.

The other element related to divorce—we mentioned space just a moment ago—concerns the difficulty people have today in conceiving that they can be committed forever. People no longer distinguish between a commitment for *always* and a commitment for *as long as possible*. They think in all sincerity that they are getting married for as long as possible. If you probe this aspect through dialogue with them, many people will tell you: "If we have problems later on, we are no better than the others, and we will do as the others do." It is implied: *We will get divorced. But this will never happen to us . . .* In reality, they have not integrated that even to say such a thing already means exposing oneself to a marriage that would be null, for the validity of a marriage is connected to this commitment, to indissolubility, to the definitive character of such a commitment for all of life. It is for always. I understand that they hesitate. One will also understand if they will have to prepare themselves in a coherent and serious manner.

In order to defend marriage, shouldn't the Church, if necessary, say, "No, I will not marry you, you are not ready"?

J.L. She does so. I have had to dissuade persons who came to see me about getting married but did not have the least intention of contracting this marriage in the meaning that the Church gives the sacrament. I also have written letters of reservation. I remember one case where the persons refused to sign the letter of intent. I could not determine from the dialogue the motivations for this refusal. I did not know whether they had reservations about what was required in the letter of intent—in which case there was absolute nullity—or if perhaps it was a matter of protesting the fact that things were demanded of them in writing. Notwithstanding, a refusal of the Church's authority was expressed clearly.

Do you believe that many ecclesiastics say no?

J.L. It happens, but rarely. Many come to see the priest to be married by him but do not want to prepare themselves, or at the very least they hardly want it. They come to see the priest, the date of the marriage is already fixed, the reception hall already is reserved, and the caterer is contracted. This raises another question: What is the freedom of the priest in this case? It is a delicate matter.

When a priest prepares fiancés, he must give himself the time to do so, and to do it in a reasonable manner. It is not a question of placing upon the fiancés the weight of such and such an idealistic vision of Christian perfection. That would not make any sense. The fact that two young baptized people want to get married in the Church means that they are exercising a legitimate right, but this right is not absolute. It is the right of each baptized person to request to be married in the Church, as no other marriage exists between two baptized persons except sacramental marriage. One cannot say on the one hand, "Your marriage is only valid if it is celebrated in the Church," and at the same time, "No, you will not get married in the Church." These are the two limits. Between the necessity to prepare the two spouses well and the legitimate right that they have to get married, there is a reasonable space. Concretely speaking: several meetings that are spaced out over at least six months, for a serious preparation in which essential questions will be addressed.

The preparation must be spiritual. If it is not, it is merely a formality. Young fiancés will go to see the more or less kind priest. They must pass through that way; the Church demands it. And they leave again into the life of the nonpracticing baptized person. It is terrible, it is a very sorrowful incoherence to be married in the Church and then not to go and render honor to God on the Sunday that follows. A sacrament has been asked of the Church. At times, the couple demands that this sacrament be celebrated in the form of a Eucharist, for it is more festive. And afterward, they neglect the Eucharist; they don't need it anymore. Afterward, when difficulties arise, if the couple has not lived with the means of grace, these problems overwhelm everything. Human nature does not always have the capacity to overcome trials, but there is great strength in persons who practice their faith in truth. There are, let us not forget to say, thousands and even hundreds of thousands of Christian families who remain faithful and who pass, even they, through difficulties.

The thing is possible. It is difficult when one looks across all of life, but that's an abstract way of looking at it. A life is one day lived after another, one month after another, a series of events that never arise at the same time. There is a grace of the state of life for married persons, as for persons who are consecrated in celibacy. This is what we must help people understand.

Another point. Young people often say, "In the past, the common life lasted for twenty years, maximum thirty years. Now, it is sixty years." An abstraction is present there; when one lives together for twenty years, why would one not live twenty-one years together? And what is that factor which proves that what was possible for twenty-one years is no longer possible for twenty-two years? The idea does not hold. If you are not capable of living together for sixty years, you aren't capable of living together for twenty years, either! During the normal life of people who grow older and continue to love each other, sixty years is like ten, twenty, or forty years. How many people are there today who think about beginning their life again at forty-five, holding on to the illusion of having an entire life in front of them? I know many cases of people who raised two or three children and who then left the family home at the age of fifty; in reality, it is not more difficult to live fifty years with one person than to live twenty years. One could imagine—in a similar vision— priests at ten years, twenty years . . . It is the opposite of a serious commitment, and it is an illusion that many young people have, because they do not have adults to explain to them why it is an illusion.

Do they have good models, for example grandparents?

J.L. Yes, but in their eyes, grandparents belong to an older time when one would remain all one's life with the same spouse.

We are the first generation who no longer give importance to the issue of living together for life with one's husband or one's wife; who fundamentally no longer desire this, even when people get married. Even so, you make a good point: Until now, they have had in front of them the example of fidelity of their grandparents, and they have not recognized in them the example of true life.

FOUR

Free Love and
Free Love in God:
Fidelity and Freedom

If we are faithless, He remains faithful—for He cannot deny
himself.

(2 TIM. 2:13)

And this is love, that we follow His commandments.

(2 JOHN 1:6)

Pierre and Véronique Sanchez: *Christianity today falls vic-*
tim, in the eyes of the general public, to profound errors committed
throughout the past by the Magisterium, and currents of thought
such as Jansenism and Puritanism. Benedict XVI has described the
situation in this manner:

> *Admittedly, forms of rigorism have also repeatedly gained*
> *ground in Christianity, and the tendency toward negative*
> *appraisals of sexuality, a tendency that had developed in*
> *Gnosticism, also found its way into the Church. Just think of*
> *Jansenism, which warped and intimidated people. It is evident*

today that we need to find our way back to the genuinely Christian attitude that existed among the first Christians and in the
great periods of Christian culture: the attitude of joy in, and affirmation of, the body, of sexuality—seen as a gift that always
requires discipline and responsibility as well.[18]

Could you return to these two notions of discipline and responsibility? How are they related to each other?

Bishop Jean Laffitte: A clarification is needed to answer
this question: The Magisterium as such has not conveyed a
pessimistic view of man and has not committed error. It has
emphasized successively some realities according to the times.
Permit me to say that in the joy you mention, of the beginnings
of the Church, of Christian hope, of the enthusiasm that existed
then, there also were very great demands placed upon Christian
conduct. It would be naïve to imagine a joy at the beginnings
while imagining that the Church never emphasized moral demands that sometimes were extremely accentuated. Remember
the instructions of Saint Paul, the Fathers of the Church, and
the practice of public penances; the importance given to the offense of adultery, and to irremittable sins that required a lifelong
penance. There was no period of immense joy, followed by a
period of austerity under Jansenism before total liberation. We
must pay attention: During the periods of dynamism and enthusiasm, the gravity of the Christian life also was present. In those
circumstances, Christians faced persecution until the very end,
sometimes up to death. It bore witness to the Resurrection of
Christ and also refused to apply pagan customs within its daily

---

18 Pope Benedict XVI, *Light of the World*, p. 103.

life. There was a consistency across the Christian life and its demands that is rich in teachings for today.

Within the field of human love and sexuality, as in other fields, discipline is the means for exercising responsibility. Discipline is never a goal. On the other hand, responsibility is an attitude of the entire person before a good worthy of being respected. At its root, it is the exercise of personal freedom in the face of a familial, social, spiritual, or ecclesial good that the person esteems worthy of being honored, served, and preserved. Responsibility presupposes a personal path and, precisely, the care for a good worthy of being received, and this touches upon personal conduct, on the exercise of a discipline. One can give an example: If you hold that a scientific, or theological, or spiritual subject, or even an art, is worthy of being studied or exercised in a profound way, you will get down to work, to labor. This presupposes a discipline for ordering the knowledge that one will acquire. If you hold that it is important for each member of your family to be able to live in a harmonious fashion, to be respected in life and in their efforts, then at the heart of your house and of your family, a certain number of practical requirements will have to be respected. Each person will be invited to respect the freedom of the other, his intimacy, his goods. Discipline is the means that one can exercise upon oneself, and upon those for whom one has charge, to be responsible. Discipline is never an end in itself.

Within the domain of sexuality and of human love, discipline must be inspired by a spiritual value, by a virtue. There is no discipline in that domain which is cut off from its virtuous root. For example, in matters of sexuality, discipline is connected to the virtue of chastity. Discipline has a root in the heart of man; if not, discipline would be a military regulation. Military discipline certainly has its usefulness, but in another register: to codify the organization of a group in view of a particular activity that consists of defending one's country. For everything that touches upon personal conduct, relations with other people, the just wage for an activity, and attention to the poor, there is a virtuous root: justice. Well, for sexuality, it is the virtue of chastity that, like all of the virtues, is connected to freedom.

In the free-loving life of today, desire often trumps love, and in any case, if the partners feel that they are in love, they are perfectly autonomous in their honey bubble; they are not indebted to anyone and must develop an overactive imagination in order for their relation to be as exciting as magazines promise them. Christian love as such does not instrumentalize the other in the service of individual pleasure. It also does not limit itself to emotions that give today's lovers the illusion of being masters of what they are feeling. To love in a Christian manner is not to set one's heart on another being, investing oneself in grasping one's desire. Could you speak to us of the relationship between desire and love?

J.L. The entire human being is fundamentally a being of desire. Desire belongs to the nature of man and of woman. Desires are very diverse, and of every nature according to their object. There are physical, bodily, and affective desires, as well as intellectual and spiritual desires. When one speaks of desire within love, this desire necessarily must be respected and, in order to respect the nature of man and of woman, it must integrate the totality of its components. The legitimate desire present in human love, of the wife toward her husband and of the husband toward his wife, must integrate all of the dynamisms of the person: bodily, affectively, and also spiritually, since we are speaking of a human love fulfilled in marriage. At that moment, what is at work is what John Paul II called "the truthful integration of love and desire." All of the elements of desire integrate and order themselves according to a hierarchy that makes spiritual desire the factor which integrates the other desires. Sexual desire is a legitimate desire and beautiful to the degree that it is tied to the affective dimension of desire for the presence of the other and for union with that person; each person also will find his flowering within the desire for spiritual encounter with the other, who never ceases to be a free subject. I think often of the magnificent text of Tobias and Sarah where one sees the spouses praying to God before uniting together: "And now, O Lord, I am not taking this sister of mine because of lust, but with sincerity. Grant that I may find mercy and may grow old together with her" (Tob. 8:7).

There is a "truthful integration," according to the expression of Blessed John Paul II. The current Pope employs another term: He speaks of the "purification" of *eros* by *agape*. This concerns at its core an interpenetration of all of the dynamisms ordered by the demands of the spirit and soul within the one who loves. This is why love cannot be reduced to sexuality, nor the latter left out of the equation, except within the context of a communal choice for a higher reason in particular cases. All of the dynamisms of the person are harmonized and integrated in a truthful manner. Karol Wojtyła already used this term within his work *Love and Responsibility*, when he was studying each of these dynamisms.

Benedict XVI attempts to read the signs of the times:

We find here in the West, too, a revival of new Catholic initiatives that are not ordered by a structure or a bureaucracy. The bureaucracy is spent and tired. These initiatives come from within, from the joy of young people. Christianity is perhaps

acquiring another face and, also, another cultural form. It does
not hold the command post in world opinion; others rule there.
But it is the vital force without which even the other things
would not continue. In this regard, thanks to what I myself am
able to see and experience, I am quite optimistic that Christian-
ity is on the verge of a new dynamic.[19]

Do you see this dynamic at work within the domain of the family?
Could you give us concrete examples, and not only from the West?

J.L. We have talked enough of a healthy preparation for
marriage to recognize that today there are a very great number
of couples and families who are, at the Christian level, truly exemplary. When I say "exemplary," I don't mean simply the fact
that they may be considered to be examples at the ethical level
or in their religious practice but rather, I would say, at the level
of personal, conjugal, and familial commitment, of holiness, for
them and for their children. These couples and families are very
often involved in larger spiritual communities, in which they
encourage each other in fraternal charity, values of solidarity,
mutual help, apostolic work, and evangelization. In my opinion,
one of the great riches—and also a new development—is the
desire of truly Christian families to evangelize. This is something very present today. As Secretary of the Pontifical Council
for the Family, I am in contact with associations within numerous countries. I can say that I regularly have the opportunity of
encountering families that truly are committed and at times are
very far along the way of personal sanctification. There is something new at work here, to the extent that they are not satisfied
merely by a Christian duty accomplished in all good conscience,

---

19 Pope Benedict XVI, *Light of the World*, p. 59.

but they are even more animated by the desire to witness to the presence of Christ living in their midst, to make Him known and to transmit Him.

Families thus have become subjects of evangelization. Very often in the past, the family was considered an *object* of evangelization, requiring the pastoral commitment of the Church and of pastors. That has not stopped being the case, and all of our conversation is centered on the need to help families to "become what they are," according to the words that conclude the post-synodal exhortation *Familiaris Consortio* of 1981: "Family, become what you are," exhorted John Paul II. Today, however, one sees more and more families who, profoundly evangelized, carry the witness of the Christian life beyond their limits. This is a reality that gives the Christian life its true features: it communicates a "taste" for God's presence, the love of the person of Christ. This is very present within conjugal and family spirituality, as it is lived across numerous continents and countries. We must seek out such people, ask them to express themselves, give them the means for apostolic action; and it would also be good if pastors encourage and assist them along this way. I have numerous examples of this. I think of the Philippines, South Korea, numerous countries in Africa, several countries in Latin America. and also, by the grace of God, several places in Europe and the Middle East.

But Christians remain the minority. Why are we so few, who understand that the laxity of the West wounds the family? What are the effects of the trivialization of pornography on the Internet? Are Christians armed against this scourge?

J.L. Families of today, and young people in particular, are confronted by totally new difficulties, such as the immediate access to all sorts of images and shows that they do not have the time to sort out or to keep at bay. There is something truly harmful to the sensitivity of persons, their modesty, and the respect for others and of their intimacy. Christian families have access to the same sources as all of the rest of society; they are confronted by this difficulty that generates tensions within the bosoms of families, among adolescents in particular, and between the parents themselves. Families are unable to rise up against the very existence of technologies that also have their positive side, but they always can give the witness of responsible Christians: They make it a rule then not to allow the sensitivity of their children to be wounded, or for the presence of God to be lost in their heart. Words of counsel, and sometimes of authority, must be presented: We really have to defend Christians for whom we have charge within our families, especially the younger ones, from that which wounds their interiority. This happens by way of the discipline that we have mentioned. One does not allow a television to be in a child's room. One can also exercise a discreet vigilance vis-à-vis adolescents when they attend social forums. Through the management of means of communication, one seeks to prevent them from falling into the slavery of immediacy, or into dependencies that are all the more ferocious, as they often pass unnoticed.

In certain cases, these means of communication allow Christians to mobilize themselves, for example against an unjust law, or to inform themselves, to invite others to gatherings, or to transmit news. However, in general, the path is most often passive; and the risk then is real that young people and children may be defenseless in the face of images that reach them.

In regard to this educating role of parents, and from a spiritual perspective, I would like to conclude with a text of Father Caffarel

on the family as a Eucharistic place: "As the priest, at the Offertory
of the Mass, presents the bread that will be consecrated by sacramental words and will become the Body of Christ, similarly parents
offer the child whom the words and water of baptism consecrate
and make the child become the child of God: It is an offertory of the
home."[20] An offering of each and every day.

J.L. There is, in effect, a Eucharistic dimension within this
offering, in the sense that Father Caffarel has shown. There also
is another classical meaning: It is the fact that, when a child is
born in a Christian family, it is a being entrusted by God, one
who belongs to God. In offering him Christian instruction and
education, parents witness constantly that he is a gift of God.
There is thus an offering that is renewed and which makes it
such that the parents cannot keep the child for themselves, that
they cannot make him a prisoner of the family cell or of the
family home, even if this home is a cozy and pleasant cocoon . . .

Up until twenty-five years old . . .

J.L. And well beyond! Sometimes until forty years old. You
know that it is a societal fact, and in Italy sociological studies
have been conducted on this precise question. But we sidetrack
from the subject!

If the child has been received by the parents as a gift of God,
a gift that does not stop belonging to Him, then they offer him
continually to God. At the core, their education expresses a recognition of this belonging. At the Offertory of the Mass, one
offers to God the work of men: "Through your goodness we have

---

20 Text cited in Louis de Raynal, *La Bonne Nouvelle du Mariage: Le Père Caffarel,
Prophète pour Notre Temps*. L'Echelle de Jacob, 2011, p. 131.

this bread to offer." We have received from God, and we present it to God so that it may become the Body of Christ. There is something profoundly Eucharistic in this domain: One offers to God a gift that He has made for us. One finds within the Magisterium of the Church older traces of this idea, for example in Leo XIII and Pius XI. Educating a child is, in some manner, to give a new son to the Kingdom; it is to enrich the Kingdom of God himself. It is extraordinary as an idea. The choice to welcome a child, to give him a Christian education, to baptize him in the death and Resurrection of Christ, is to give one child more to the Church. The communion of saints will be enriched by the presence of these children in Heaven! That provides momentum when one is Christian.

FIVE

Two Names of Fidelity: Obedience and Authority

Pierre and Véronique Sanchez: *I return to a fact that perhaps has not been discussed enough: "A new heart I will give you, and a new spirit I will put within you; and I will take out of your flesh the heart of stone and give you a heart of flesh. And I will put my spirit within you, and cause you to walk in my statutes and be careful to observe my ordinances. You shall dwell in the land which I gave to your fathers; and you shall be my people, and I will be your God" (Ezek. 36:26–28). We always come back to it in the Bible, in the Covenant: God is faithful, and man responds to Him by being obedient. We notice as well that in this verse, it is God Himself who makes us obedient and will help us to be obedient. As if God put His own obedience within us!*

Bishop Jean Laffitte: What is in its seminal form in this passage from Ezekiel finds its fulfillment within the mystery of the Passion of Christ. He fulfills exactly what obedience is, obedience to His Father. And by this mystery of His death, of His Resurrection and of the gift of the Holy Spirit, He renders our humanity—each one of us—capable of obedience each in his turn. It is no longer only the fact that God helps us through an assistance that may be conceived as a timely, exterior help, as happens in the Old Testament: God is omnipotent; He has every capacity to help us.

In the New Testament, Christ makes Himself obedient even unto death. In order to understand the nature of obedience, we must enter into this path of Christ. What is the type of obedience that Christ manifests toward the Father? In fact, it is a disposition of the heart, a bond of union with the Father and His plan, a bond of cordial, total, interior, and profound adherence. The human will of Christ is one with the divine will. All of Jesus' being in His humanity adheres to the Father's plan, a plan for the salvation of all men. It so happens that the salvation of men passes through this offering of Christ in His humanity. He shows us the obedience that we are called to have toward the Father: adhering to His plan, to His will, seen not from the outset as a norm exterior to our will or to our intelligence, but as a kind of interior, spiritual, and loving persuasion. Within the Heart of Christ, there is no rejection of the Father's authority. Certainly His conscious humanity is overcome as it moves toward its annihilation; we remember Christ's cry of abandonment: "My God, my God, why have You abandoned me?" (Matt. 27:46; Ps. 22:2). The expression of a human nature is present there, meaning not a human nature that revolts, but one that cannot yet fully grasp this mystery, for this mystery is inaccessible. Even so, through His will, Christ is united to the plan and will of the Father. There is a kind of annihilation: He will be crushed on the Cross, but obedience is always there, an interior movement filled with humble and filial love.

What is remarkable is that the model of obedience that Christ teaches us is not obedience to a boss, or to an emperor, a governing minister, or an executive manager; it is a filial obedience to His Father. This filial quality in fact is a most inspiring model of obedience for the human relationships between parents and children.

If the "authors" of our days—namely, our parents—want to be faithful to their status and responsibility as parents, they have the duty to exercise their "authority" over us in order to help us to grow. As the etymology of the word illustrates, there is an intrinsic link between procreation and authority. Why is such a simple thing not better understood in our culture?

J.L. There certainly are several elements that shed light upon this development. The authority of parents no longer is perceived as natural, in spite of the real bond that you point out between authority and parents. The sole fact today of possibilities for procreation outside of the exclusive bond between the mother and the father—let us think of the diffusion of all the methods of artificial fertilization—leads to undervaluing the symbolic weight of the parents' role. When procreation takes place outside of the joint presence of two parents, or occurs simply because of an individual's desire to have a child outside any context of a family founded upon marriage, the result is that, in a certain way, parents cease to be those who alone generate human life. Accordingly, the child at times becomes the mere extension of a desire for a child, for fatherhood or for motherhood. He no longer is appreciated for what he is naturally: the fruit of the love of a man and a woman who belong to each other, who are united, and who are his parents.

The entire meaning of fatherhood and motherhood is challenged. If one separates the biological phenomenon of procreation from its parental origin and its ultimate purpose, then one no longer can perceive that bringing children into the world creates a responsibility and confers an authority.

As Benedict XVI reminds us, it is without a doubt within the notion of responsibility that love and law succeed in coming together: "The same thing applies here that applies everywhere: Freedom and responsibility belong together. For only then does real joy also grow, is a real Yes possible. This underscores the importance of setting forth afresh, as something positive, as a great affirmation, the Christian image of man."[21] One is far from being superhuman. Could you return to this affirmation which, according to Benedict XVI, is neither a debasement nor a degradation?

J.L. The term *affirmation* is extremely well chosen: It is a kind of submission of intelligence and of heart to a rationality and goodness that exceeds them. It is a movement that is natural. Far from cutting off our freedom, this affirmation is in its depths a cordial assent. We experience love, and we discover that this love may be referred to a greater love that exceeds us: the love of God for us. We adhere to it, for we know that unlike the love that we experience for one person, this love of God for us is all-powerful and infinitely patient: a totally sacrificial love that opens up to life, to the transcendent, and to all that helps man's faculties reach their full potential.

God's love goes as far as the gift of His divine life, let us not forget! There is on the one hand the gift that Christ makes of His life on the Cross, and there also is this gift of the Holy Spirit that aims to make us adoptive children. The gift of the Holy Spirit makes us children of God, or "gods," as the Fathers of the Church said. We cannot but affirm this, for, in this adherence, we find not only our greatest happiness but also our natural happiness that seeks to unfold, to spread, and to arise in a manner that one would not suspect. There is nothing in common

---

21 Pope Benedict XVI, *Light of the World*, p. 103.

between the fact of simply loving with our mere natural strength and loving with the strength that God gives to His friends.

This applies from the time of engagement and continues within marriage. Could you comment and perhaps recall the masculine counterpart that so often is ignored? I am referring to the precept of Saint Paul that is so misunderstood: "Women, be submissive to your husbands." Equality in the republican sense of the term is mechanical, but Christianity manages to conceive equality within contrast and complementarity. How does it manage this?

J.L. Within the economy of the children of God, Christianity does not consist of making equals in the sense that persons would be interchangeable. There are only unique persons. Thus there can be no imaginary or ideological equality there. The equality that exists between the children of God is an equality of dignity. It is not an equality of gifts or of talents, or of histories, patrimony, or family, but of dignity. Each person has been wanted by God and is loved infinitely by Him. This is the truthful equality between men.

With this as our starting point, the question of submission is a question that each person naturally is brought to live vis-à-vis this source of love and of goodness that is God. There is something that corresponds to masculine *and* feminine human nature. Men are not at all excluded from the affirmation of which we have spoken, from the submission of which Saint Paul spoke. When Saint Paul speaks of the submission of wives to their husbands, he speaks of it within a context that places in relief the care that the man must have for his wife: to love her as his own body. He loves his wife, he protects her, he takes care of her. John Paul II proposes an interpretation that is radically new in the history of discussing Saint Paul's passage when he speaks of a "reciprocal submission." Approximately ten years ago, a doctoral thesis in Biblical theology traced the history of interpretation of the verse and demonstrated the novelty of this reading by John Paul II. It concerns a submission that does not take on the same form in the man and in the woman.

Our secularized society has ended up casting authority and obedience outside of their frames of reference. Marxism chose this path also, and imposed the rudimentary outline of its own relationships of alienating powers. Instead, Scripture proposes to us an idea of obedience and authority that has nothing to do with reductive simplicity. There can be a relationship of authority and obedience within love. Jesus even goes much further, since he says: "My food is to do the will of Him who sent me" (John 4:34). In the same way, the Our Father juxtaposes the two following invocations: "May Your will be done on earth as in Heaven" and "Give us this day our daily bread." As if obedience is nourishing?

J.L. One could take a further step in relation to what we said earlier concerning the act of supreme obedience that Christ accomplished in our nature, an act that rendered us capable of following Him along this way. This would be to consider that His act of filial obedience is actualized, reiterated daily, by the celebration of the Eucharistic mystery. The Eucharistic sacrifice is truly the actualization of this offering and of this thanksgiving. This is why it is called a sacrifice: the renunciation of Christ's own life in an offering to the Father. In a sacramental way, this act is made nourishment: The Body and the Blood of Christ, which are the very reality of this obedience carried to its ultimate point of fulfillment and of perfection, become food and drink.

There is a radical theological connection between obedience

and nourishment. The baptized person is nourished by the obedience of Christ, as he makes it his own. He becomes obedient himself. This is neither a colorful image nor a scholarly theological development. It is the reality of the Christian life, the Eucharistic reality of the Christian life.

In this light, we can understand why we nourish ourselves in a natural way from obedience. It is because obedience refers itself to an authority. You do not obey a dictator; rather, you are subjected to his law because you do not have a choice. You are constrained physically, psychologically, to submit yourself to a rule decreed by someone, by one party, by a dominant group that does not give you the least space to adhere to it. He imposes it on you: you are not free. It is therefore not an act of obedience. An arbitrary power imposes itself by force. Authority is very different! Certainly it confers a power, but it is primary with respect to the power that it exercises. There is a whole debate that judges are familiar with: the link that exists between *auctoritas* [authority] and *potestas* [power]. There is no *potestas* without reference to an *auctoritas* that founds it.

This authority springs up, flows from the very being of the person. Thus, when Christ moves in the midst of men, He heals, and the people ask themselves by what authority He does this. The Evangelists state: "He taught them as one who had authority" (Luke 4:32; Matt. 7:29). In the same way, He spoke with authority, for his words expressed what He was. The authority of Jesus flowed from the nature of the Son of God. The people were amazed and attracted, for everything in Him led them to adhere to His words and to follow Him.

The same thing happens in people's ordinary lives. You have persons who inspire respect due to who they are, or because their acts have revealed that they are genuine. This phenomenon, moreover, has interested philosophers. Scheler, for example, studied exemplary figures of geniuses, heroes, and saints who aroused admiration in diverse ways: the genius because the limits to intelligence seem not to apply in his case; the hero because the love of the common good and of country is carried to the point of self-sacrifice; and the saint, whose love can go as far as martyrdom for the sake of Christ, because he communicates a goodness without limits, which leads him to the point of accepting his own annihilation.

In what concerns parents, they have an authority that is inherent to their state as parents. It is an authority by nature. Parents are a man and a woman who have assumed total responsibility vis-à-vis the fruit of their love. There is a child who is about to be born, who is born, who grows up as their son or their daughter. Their authority as parents expresses itself in the most worthy manner within a responsible commitment. Responsibility is at the heart of the very expression of the parents' authority. When they exercise their authority, parents demonstrate their responsibility in relation to their children. As you know, responsibility has three dimensions: who is responsible, for what is he responsible, and in front of whom? Parents are responsible for welcoming, bringing up, and educating their child: They want to give him the greatest personal, material, moral, and spiritual autonomy. This child one day will be an adult who will consider them and appreciate their fatherhood and their motherhood with the eyes of an adult. The child will remember as an adult what he received or did not receive. Finally, parents are responsible before God, the source of all life. If this child exists, it is not only because the parents carried out a very precise act; rather it is because, through the mediation of this act, the Creator intervened and created this life. The acts of union between a man and a woman are not automatically fruitful: Fertile parents do not transmit life each time they unite. He gives life at the moment chosen by Him, but it passes through this mediation that is the union of the spouses.

The parents exercise an authority whose origin they know transcends them. If they were completely to exclude this origin of life and to reject the very idea of a good Creator, then their responsibility, reduced to the horizon of this life, would be weakened.

Above all, the authority of God is benevolence: At the bosom of the conjugal love they share, the spouses nourish themselves with the love of God through prayer, and it is thanks to the Father's care that couples are able to face eventual difficulties. "Happy are those who follow His commands" (Ps. 119:2). Benedict XVI writes concerning Saint Catherine of Bologna: "She was credible in her authority, because she was able to see that for her authority meant, precisely, serving others."[22] What kind of relation between authority and service does the Church propose?

J.L. One cannot but think again of Jesus' paradoxical response to James and John, who are seeking the two greatest places in the Kingdom; Jesus directs His reply also to the other ten Apostles scandalized by such a request: "If any one would be first, he must be last of all and servant of all" (Mark 9:35). This is what Jesus did: He did not despise the condition of a slave but made Himself the servant of all. He who is at the service of all is a slave; there is no one below Him.

The service of which we are speaking is not servile. It is a loving service. I am struck by St. Paul's words to Philemon, when he sends Onesimus back to him: "Perhaps this is why he was parted from you for awhile, that you could have him back

---

22 Pope Benedict XVI, General Audience of December 29, 2010.

forever, no longer as a slave but more than a slave, as a beloved
brother; especially to me but how much more to you, both in
the flesh and in the Lord" (Philem. 1:15–16). Paul recommends
Onesimus to other Christian brethren. Why? Because this slave
served well, with respect and love. In serving, he grew, he became a brother. "No longer do I call you servants . . . but I have
called you friends" (John 15:15), Jesus says to His own. He who
serves Christ in the person of his brothers and of the littlest of
them all, makes himself a slave of all and their servant, but this
loving service may take the apparently lowest forms of service:
Recall the sanctity of Saint Martin de Porres, patron saint of
Peru, a man who was virtually illiterate and who spent his life
cleaning his monastery. He did it with such love that the people
made a habit of assembling themselves around him; between
two sweeps of the broom, he then would do catechesis. He did
nothing except love while fulfilling the most humble service,
consisting of cleaning house for his community. There is an extraordinary mystery here: the smallest has become the greatest.
Saint Martin de Porres is honored by humble people, and also by
the powerful! Certain saints left no writings, nor were they distinguished by their thinking, intelligence, or brilliant discourses,
but only by the quality of love in their service. Saint Martin
de Porres is a master who teaches us the connection between
service, love, and affirmation. But there are others like him!

*It also seems that the exercise of authority, far from being incom-
patible with love, is inseparable from it. In forbidding the fruit of the
tree of knowledge, the Lord drew the boundary between His identity
and that of His creatures. He protected men from the temptation of
excess. The Lord asks us to respect certain limits not in order to punish us, but rather to allow us to live His love in spirit and in truth.
"For God sent His Son into the world, not to condemn the world,*

but that the world might be saved through Him" (John 3:17). In the
garden of the couple, of the family, what according to you is the tree
of knowledge of good and evil?

J.L. I must take this question with a little bit of humor!
There is certainly a small forest, with trees of all kinds, large
and small. I would perhaps be as curious as Adam and Eve and
would like to know everything that each one of them offers.
Let us imagine that a tree of knowledge of the family exists! To
what does this "knowledge" refer? Knowing that the love which
motivates us, and which takes on an extraordinary expression in
fruitfulness, comes from a source greater than us. The first thing
is thus the knowledge of the source of the love that lives within
us. The second: The fruits of this love do not belong to us. We
are trustees of it. They are entrusted to us by the Master of life.
Our children do not belong to us, and yet they are truly our children! They give rise to all of our love and attention, our worries
and cares, our sufferings and joys, but these children belong to
God. God has a plan for each one of them just as He has had for
each of us, their parents.

And yet, when suffering interferes . . .

J.L. The tree of the knowledge of good and evil . . . We do
not know very well what it is. Everything is not fully known to
us. However, one thing is very certain: We cannot fathom the
mystery of God's freedom concerning others, concerning those
we love, and in particular concerning each of our own children.
Sadly, we often learn it a posteriori in suffering and pain, for example when we suddenly are deprived of the presence of someone dear to us. When parents have lived through the trial of
losing their child, they necessarily ask themselves the question

of the meaning of an existence prematurely interrupted: Is it a fulfilled life, or is there a lack of fulfillment? As Christians, we cannot believe in a fulfillment that escapes us. We do not affirm what is against nature in the death of those whom we love and the suffering that it generates. We say yes to the love of God that accomplishes all things.

On this point, it is useful to think of those people whose holiness manifested itself very early on and who departed this world very young. Nobody would think of seeing in the figure of a Saint Thérèse of Lisieux, who died at the age of only twenty-four, a holiness that was unfinished. On the contrary, we see it as normal that she is one of the patron saints of France, the patroness of missions, and even a doctor of the Church! And what are we to say of Saint Dominic Savio, who departed this life at the age of fourteen; or Saints Agatha or Agnes, martyred during their early adolescence; or, much closer to us, the young Pier Giorgio Frassati, who departed this life at the threshold of a dazzling career? And how many others are there who remain unknown? Divine Providence is sovereign, and we can only adore Him, even when His designs humanly appall us. If we doubt the love of God, we begin to place ourselves in the attitude of one who judges God. Even if we do not doubt His love, we can still question it, even sharply. Some saints were able to do so, but never blaspheming the Holy Name of God. Benedict XVI's first encyclical is completely consecrated to this theme: *Deus Caritas Est*. To say "God is love" is to allow the filial trust that we have already mentioned to grow within us.

Trust is born from benevolence. Faith roots itself in the Goodness of God, in which we cannot doubt. However, often this trust in benevolence runs up against malice.

J.L. Yes, there is another element that I would like to express. Malice raises a serious question. There is a categorical separation, an abyss—like the abyss that separates the poor Lazarus from the greedy rich man in the Gospel—that separates benevolence from malice. Everything plays out there, and this seems to me to be very important. When we are young and grow up, we have several criteria for judgment and reference. We spontaneously judge people, at times without pity. We judge those who are beautiful and those who are ugly, those who are intelligent and those who are stupid, those who are great and those who are small, those who are interesting and those who are boring. We have the tendency to make divisions without realizing how relative they are. On the other hand, there is a divide that is fundamental: that which opposes goodness and gratuitous malice. In the first place, love, the gift of self, service, and affirmation of others—to take up your expression again— are related. Secondly, jealousy, hatred, contempt for the poor, ingratitude, cynicism, and indifference toward others are linked. There is the true divide to which we always must be attentive.

Observe the reactions of Jesus: He had a delicacy of soul that made Him recognize instantly what pleased His Father, a compassion and an infinite mercy for the sick and for sinners. He always saw the good in others. At times He marveled at the faith of a Roman centurion or the attachment of Mary Magdalene, and sometimes He taught His own, encouraged them, or sent them on a mission. You will notice, however, that there were circumstances in which He became angry and showed no leniency. Those who do evil and who want evil possess an evil will that consists in desiring evil for others. There is obviously a weakness in men that can lead to specific entrance points of jealousy or malice. I speak of gratuitous malice, this "ontological malice" of which the philosopher Jankélévitch spoke, the very core of a bad freedom that is inexplicable. The events lived at the time of the Second World War led him to reflect upon the mystery of evil that overtakes us and obliges us to turn ourselves toward God to question Him. This is what a very great number of Jewish philosophers have done whose personal reflections on the mystery of evil have opened up to a theological type of questioning. We should not be astonished at all by this, since this is due truly to a human logic that cannot understand, allow, or compromise itself with gratuitous malice. Thus, there is a divide that opposes the good and the wicked. This is not a binary logic: It is the exercise of human freedom when it deliberately chooses to do good or to do evil. In this latter case, there is a denial of freedom, of its nature and therefore of its life, a denial of others and of the love of God. The choice of evil is a slope where everything is carried along as in an apocalyptic whirlwind. It is a mystery so great that thinkers can only express it through the expression of "privation of good," in order to translate this negation of being. All partial attraction toward evil is contrary to nature. There is something metaphysical in the existence of gratuitous evil. In reality, there is a moment where man can commit himself, I would not say to the service of evil, but in the slavery of evil. It is the enigma of gratuitous malice. When one has the occasion of encountering it in life or being confronted by it, it certainly is a scouring experience at the spiritual level, and at times humanly destructive. But Christ is conqueror over evil, and the Cross of Christ has vanquished the Adversary.

One often poses the question of suffering and evil, of their origin. These questions do not coincide totally. Suffering can be redemptive. As for evil, it may seem overwhelming if one forgets that it has been defeated, and definitively so, by the Savior. Jesus is the Savior.

THE CHOICE OF THE FAMILY

Many parents today abdicate their responsibility. Fewer people understand the dictum: "He who loves well chastises well." One is ashamed of taking on the bad role and the feeling of culpability that one always has, more or less, when one punishes a child. It is a contradiction in terms. It is a duty to punish a child. What do you think?

J.L. The child who transgresses and disobeys does not ever become the enemy of his parents. This is the reason why the sanction in reality is an instrument that the parents give to the child in order to help him see what distinguishes his right from his left. It is clear that we are speaking here of proportionate sanction and not the expression of their anger or impatience. It does not mean that when someone sanctions a serious fault in his child, he does not love him. However, it also must be said that as much as the child is fallible in his capacity to obey, parents are as weak in their capacity to educate and thus eventually to punish in a proportionate way. If a child has committed a grave moral fault, for example theft, that deserves distinct, on-the-spot justice and a sanction, which only the parents' tenderness allows to be measured out in a manner that still manifests their love. If one punishes a child in the same manner for a coffee stain that he has made on a clean tablecloth as for theft, then the sanction becomes ineffective. One must pay close attention. The true pedagogue is he who leads along the way. In general, things do not move toward sanction. However when sanctions come, they must be necessary and proportionate to the moral importance of what has been committed by the child, knowing that the child does not always have clear knowledge of the gravity of what he has done. An act of gratuitous cruelty toward an animal, for example, must be corrected and explained. An act of oversight must be corrected, sometimes sharply, but it is not the same thing. I believe that one must be temperate enough.

Sanction is always an act of love on the condition that it does not express the anger of the educators, but expresses instead the concern of leading the child back along the natural path that is the good. At times it is better not to sanction when you are angry. It is appropriate to make a significant distinction between transgressions that have a more or less grave, real moral impact and mistakes that all children of the world commit. Nowadays, we often witness parents failing to live up to their responsibilities when they consider wrongdoings, even grave ones, as nothing but a means to acquire maturity. This is totally false in the moral sphere.

Supposing that at times I do not carefully punish my child—in this way, the child also learns his parents' limitations at the same time as his own, and it is a fundamental apprenticeship. Nothing stops the guilty parent from asking pardon of his child. It certainly will not cause confusion in the child's mind, causing him to swing between an authoritarian father and a father who, like Father Christmas, would be too gentle. On the contrary, it is an opportunity to make the distinction with the child between shared wrongs. Often it is an opportunity for understanding further what really has happened: One may unearth the foundations, thanks to reciprocal listening. It is a concrete example that often happened at our house.

J.L. Let us hope for his sake that the child discovers the limitations of his parents in a manner different than an excess of sanctions! Your question touches on a practice that is very recommendable for family unity, that of reconciliation. There too, a certain prudence is in order. Parents do not have to ask pardon of their children for every raising of the voice that has been a little higher than average. However, there are circumstances where asking pardon has proven to be very necessary. If they do not do so, a wound can form that may stay for a very long time. I am thinking in particular of unjust sanctions.

Among the wounds inflicted upon children that are the worst to heal, we may include, as a matter of fact, the harms caused by unjustly imposed punishments. One sometimes must be accountable for blunders in expression toward a child. In the case of punishment for a fault that he did not commit, it is good that the parents recognize that they have made a mistake. A child accused falsely remembers it for his entire life, and that can change a mechanism of authority in him that he will exercise in relation to his own children thirty years later. There is an equivalent phenomenon at work when a child perceives that one of his parents has lied to him. When a child discovers that his father or his mother has a double life, for example, it is a terrible drama to him because his moral compass is devastated. When children discover at twelve or thirteen years old that nothing they have been taught has been lived, it is psychologically and spiritually devastating. Priests and therapists, at a later stage, sometimes see the damage.

In family life, there are extreme cases, but there are very healthy practices in daily life. First of all, there is prayer in the family. But it is good that this prayer before going to bed be concluded by actions that the family members carry out in order to greet or to wish one another a good night, kissing as a sign of reconciliation. Do not allow the sun to set on a disagreement.

J.L. Everything relies upon the parents' ability to discern. A child is educated with love, but one mustn't bring to mind all of his shortcomings and failures. Certain faults are due to the fact that we are dealing with a weak being, still growing, who does not yet have adult knowledge. In my opinion, there are many points that must not be taken up again, even if there are essential things to which one must always return. For the rest, everything is a question of proportion and judgment. One therefore must distinguish what is grave and what is less so. We note as well that each family has its own dynamic and history. In order to finish this topic, I believe that children also must be educated to have a solidarity between them: One who tells on another must not have an interest in doing so. He will stop enjoying tattletaling when he shares the punishment of the child who has transgressed.

Authority comes from nature, but also from the Christian and moral spiritual coherence of personal conduct and reliability of the parents. When children know that they can trust in their parents, the rest follows . . . naturally, with the grace of God!

All couples know also from experience how an exchange that is a bit stormy between spouses often clears the air and brings back blue skies. It is strange that we would fear so much those expressions of affection that are a bit vigorous, even violent, precisely in the midst of an overall environment of aggression against which nobody protests. Is anger not at times a source of freedom?

J.L. There is an unrealistic and idealistic vision of human concord and of harmony that shuns all harshness of language and all lively expressions of a conviction, systematically avoiding all contradictory exchanges. This does not correspond at all to the dynamism of communion people live within the human condition. One must not be offended by the fact that a profound, sincere, and real love may at times know difficult moments. For example, one difficulty can come from the fact that a choice appears to be very clear for one of the two parents, while the other is full of doubt, as for example concerning the choice of a particular educational institution. That there might be exchanges lively in tone, nothing would be more normal. Once someone has had this reality check, he can attain a superior realism and can consider that in reality, the expression of a conviction in too lively a way can wound, due to the fact that we find ourselves in a weak condition. One then avoids expressing his own conviction so heatedly. It is a kind of oscillation within the normal acceptance of the texture of everyday life with all of its defects, its ups and downs; but at the same time, there is this absolute concern not to wound the sensitivity of the other. The inevitable character of such conflicts must not lead to an attitude where one gives free reign to this tendency . . . In certain cases, it suffices to wait a day before speaking again about a problem, and everything happens in the greatest tranquility.

If one returns to the beginning of my response—that is to say, concerning this current view where everything has to go well, whatever the circumstances may be—we realize that often the truth causes fear: We love the other to the degree that he does not bother us in asserting his opinions. We are in a civilization where we don't like being disturbed by the other. I remember this thought of Maritain: "It is not because one has a weak thought that one necessarily has a tender heart. And it is not because one has a vigorous thought that one has a hard heart." May we therefore have firm and vigorous thought, with the most loving and tender heart possible.

The language of the body (in the dimension of love as well as within the dimension of authority) seems to have lost its meaning: Eroticism has been severed from its living source of love, and a lot of parents do not dare crack down, because without knowing it, they are terrified by their own violence, which they fear they can't control. Could the family not be the place for a reeducation

in this language of the body, of which all of society would be the
beneficiary?

J.L. With respect to the bodily dimension, we never hear
of education with respect to one's own body and the bodies of
others. The family is a very great school for an apprenticeship in
personal dignity, not in prudery, rigorism, or fear, but in respect
for the intimacy of others. This is very important in my opinion,
especially among siblings: Never enter a room without knocking, respect each other's room when the parents are able to offer
separate rooms (which is not always the case) . . . These indi-
cations make good sense. John Paul II often raised the theme
of modesty, upon which he established a catechesis showing
how it ensures the protection of personal dignity and the body.
Modesty has a great role to play, as it is a personal defense of
one's own intimate depths. In every person, what appears, what
is known of him, his face, his profile, his hands, always leaves
intact the mystery of his depths. The intimacy of one's body has
great importance. In all cultures, there are codes for the protection of persons, of this intimacy and then of respect for the
other's mystery in what he holds most secret. The body must not
cease expressing the person in who he is, his personality.

The current crisis of the family and of marriage is closely related
to the modern crisis of authority. This is a complex and difficult
phenomenon that contains a labyrinth of multiple factors, notably
the persistent influence of Marxist ideology, which does not recognize
persons as Christianity does, and which sees relationships in terms of
power. A certain feminism, in the inherited makeup of these currents
of thought, has caused damage within the institution of the family.
What do you think concerning the status of women and mothers of
families today?

J.L. It is a delicate question; I am convinced that the Church alone has considered this issue with the seriousness it requires, in order to analyze it in a balanced way. For example, she has dedicated an important text to the dignity of the woman. The Church takes into account the new demands that are made of women, but along a pathway that does not abolish the difference between a man and a woman. You know that feminism developed in its secular perspective within the Anglo-Saxon culture about 150 years ago, and it expressed itself dialectically while professing to abolish all differences in the choices of life, children, and professional activities. One often forgets that one of the metamorphoses of this unilateral idea of feminism is that it was put into practice within the totalitarian system of Soviet communism, as within Chinese communism. In these systems, women were and still are called to carry out extremely demanding professions at the physical level. Women were doing work that demanded a lot of strength, managing very heavy machinery. Has that resulted in women's liberation? Obviously not. Within this condition imposed by these totalitarian regimes, women were not free to have children. I remind you that the significant problem of post-Soviet Russia is a demographic problem. Women who were introduced into difficult professional activities were led not to have children; each time a child announced its presence, one responded with an abortion. On average, each woman in Russia has had several abortions. We have a country, Russia, that loses roughly 900,000 persons each year while the number of abortions annually totals more than 1.5 million (according to the official numbers). The caricature of a feminism founded on equality of power has led women to the impossibility of welcoming children.

Is there a more balanced feminism? Yes. The Church demands absolute respect for the dignity of the woman. As time goes on, new demands have appeared. The legitimate desire for a woman to have a profession, to study, or to work is a point to consider, as is her profound desire and aspiration to live out conjugal, familial, and maternal values. The problem lies there: What importance does one place on and acknowledge concerning this aspiration of women to harmonize a conjugal and familial life with professional demands? Numerous women desire to raise children and to devote to them all of the time necessary during the first years of their existence. When considered in all of its dimensions, respect for the dignity of the woman demands clear recognition—including serious economic measures—of a mother's activity when she cares for her children and must put her professional activity on hold for a number of years.

What the woman does in her home is for the benefit of all society: she is not asking for a societal structure to do it in her place. The question of evaluating and politically recognizing this contribution should be a politically essential issue. The adjustment of work times is also an important avenue. A woman should be able to have the choice of having the children that she desires. She should not be constrained to renounce this fundamental desire of being a mother for practical reasons of economic or financial insufficiency imposed by the State. One observes how countries that are enjoying a less catastrophic demographic situation than others are those that have maintained substantial aid to families through the provision of family benefits. We could speak for a very long time of each European country's demography while analyzing the aid put in place for families. In Italy, this type of assistance is nearly nonexistent, and the country has had an extremely worrying demographic winter for thirty-five years. The Church is working while reflecting on these questions; it is one of the tasks of the Pontifical Council for the Family.

According to this logic, we could raise the question of mothers who work and return home late. Children are left to themselves in front of television screens, or they loiter in the street.

J.L. It's all one. Family life is a balance. Adjustments may be made as needed, including new needs. One cannot refuse a need because it is new in relation to other necessities that existed in the past! One simply must avoid that which endangers the global balance of the family. You have persons who work three hundred kilometers from their home! If parents work two hours away from their home, if the father of a family works in Paris while living in Lyon or Dijon, that creates a very precarious family balance. Such a situation might be understandable for one or two years. However, a habitual life constructed around such an anomaly would seem very problematic at an anthropological level.

The same question arises for both parents. If their mother returns home late, what do the children do? It is good to prioritize choices. Nobody objects to the legitimacy of unilaterally choosing to pursue a career while disregarding the other dimensions of life. It is a personal choice. However, the choice to establish a family demands consistency. One is able to combine several things, at the cost of eventual sacrifices, but not contradictory things. It is necessary to reflect concretely upon and to see the thresholds of tolerance within this domain. People accept commuting for one hour in the morning and evening. They find a precarious balance, but they do it. That's one thing. But is it good for someone to commute for two hours in the morning and two hours in the evening if he or she is responsible for a family? The question must be asked in these terms. In certain countries, one witnesses families torn apart for economic reasons: The woman stays in her country with the children, and the father carries out a professional activity in another country, only returning home once a year. It cannot be said that the family balance has won out in this case!

Without judging these situations . . .

J.L. Of course. Who can make a judgment when he is not in the position of having responsibility for a couple or family? It is not a question of judging either persons or the choices they make. It's simply underscoring that, among the components of family life, there are things that threaten the balance of the family and the couple. It is good to evaluate them and to try to remedy them. The prudential judgment of families must be combined with parental concern for their children and economic and financial needs.

Yes, people often say: "I do not have any choice." However, one perceives that they do not wish to make sacrifices in their level of comfort.

J.L. Everything lies in knowing: What does one desire most deeply? One cannot have one hundred great desires at a time and satisfy them all. Within the heart of man, there is room for desire of the infinite, but there is no room for an infinity of desires! When one has the choice of a husband or wife, when there are children, it is a fundamental choice due to the responsibility we mentioned. Activity serves also to make the competence of a person fruitful, but it is subordinated to the support of the family and not only to personal self-realization. This is where the choice is made, at the moment where contradictory trends appear. What do I choose to sacrifice, to adjust, to make a priority? It is all a question of judgment.

You speak well when you say that "education is an accompaniment, and not violence." In education, one cannot separate the role of each of the parents, and I quote you: "Human fatherhood and motherhood complete each other, to the point that their respective roles are exercised decisively in turn." How do you see the distribution of roles of authority in order that the children, little by little, discover their own personal identity?

J.L. This is a question that raises a number of issues of an anthropological nature. Fundamentally, the child needs his parents, and his two parents together. This being said, according to the ages of development, he needs predominantly one or the other parental figure.

Here is a classic example: The child who is born has need for the security that only his mother can give him, for she prolongs the complete security that he had within the maternal womb. The fact of having been separated from her at the moment of birth comes to be integrated into his person throughout the course of his first months after birth. During these months, the child does not distinguish spontaneously between his body and that of his mother. This is the reason why he feeds himself from his mother . . . There is a fundamental need to be in her arms, for he needs this physical and affective contact. The time comes, which varies according to the particular person, when the child is confronted by the figure of the father. At the psychological level, if the mother is a security figure, the father is a figure of authority and the moral norm. During the first months, the father is perceived as a rival: It is he who has rights to the mother. The child discovers that his rights vis-à-vis the mother are not infinite. He discovers another figure who has rights in relation to his mother. It is a process that transpires sometimes in a painful manner, yet the child must integrate it; it is a very important stage for the structuring of the personality. When this occurs in a normal and natural fashion—in the majority of cases and very early on, between one and a half to two years—the child then assimilates the figures of both parents by distinguishing them; he integrates the fact that his two parents are together, walking in step and both forming the authority to which he refers. When he begins to babble "papa" or "mama," when he has his first experience of socializing with brothers and sisters and then at school, he will say "my parents" very quickly or "my dad and my mom." He associates them. The child refers to his two parents.

When he grows up, the child needs the structuring presence of his father. The confidence that his father gives him, and the little secrets that he shares with him, will build him up. This process will prevent the child from referring constantly to the mother because she always offers security. Children who grow up need the help alternately more of a father or of a mother. A young girl who transforms at the moment of adolescence certainly has a need in particular for her mother. The young boy who grows up must face his father, who is a little bit of a rival in whose presence the boy begins to notice his own flaws: He is less sportive than his father, he does not understand much concerning new technologies . . . and his father is always older! But what matters is not to have a fusional agreement on everything, but that the child is able to speak freely to each of his parents, to express himself freely in return for lessons and advice. There is nothing more unbearable than parents who are sanctimoniously holier-than-thou moralizers. Children must not hear unceasingly "you have to" and "you must." It is good that they hear it at times, but not ceaselessly. Adolescents often say, "Allow me to breathe. I know what I have to do." Adolescents do not always know what they have to do, but they must say this. Common sense, indeed a lot of good sense, is necessary for raising children.

Authority and obedience lead us to a discussion of pardon and hence to sin. The French motto that decorates the pediments of our city halls—and sometimes even our cathedrals—stamped during the French Revolution with "Liberté Egalité Fraternité" is no longer understood by contemporary democracy according to its originally Christian meaning. We have problems conceiving equality within asymmetry and, for the majority of people among us, a very hard time imagining that the exercise of authority can be a manifestation of love. We reject the notion of original sin; we no longer speak of feeling guilty in order to clear guilt away. There is this habit of freeing people from guilt at all cost, a denial of original sin that in reality shows a profound need for pardon. What do you think of this?

J.L. You mention our French Republican trilogy. If we were truly to take seriously what each of these terms also signifies according to its Christian meaning, we would be very surprised. We have spoken already of the freedom of God's children, one that is not an arbitrary freedom to do whatever we want, whenever we want. We have spoken of equality while specifying that it has to do with an equality of dignity among God's children. However, we never speak today of the third term: *Fraternity.* We never speak of it, and even those who belong to philosophical schools of thought that use the term *brother* speak of it in a hidden way. It is only within the Church that the baptized call each other "brothers" in front of the world, and not in a hidden fashion, taking up this fraternal bond that exists between men by the fact that they are children of God.

Let us return to the principal subject of the question: pardon. Asking for pardon is seen as debasement and degradation.

If the world does not accept love in its grandeur, in its demanding nature, and in its purity, *a fortiori* it will not accept that
which is an expression of love: pardon. As you know, the word
pardon comes from the Latin *perdonum*, which means "perfect
gift." The prefix *per* expresses an accomplishment, a perfecting.
Pardon is a perfect love: It is the love that God practices.

It is within this context that one understands the profound
meaning of the original fault that all men have inherited. In
their nature, something has distorted their relationship with
God and with other men. The relationship with God ceased to
be spontaneous, trusting, made up of approval and obedience,
in all of the meanings we have mentioned before. At the core,
the relationship with God would be transformed if man were to
accept the fact that God pardons him. The problem is not that
there may be a God who pardons and a man who may be pardoned. The problem is the obstacle to pardon in him who does
not want it, conceive of it, or ask God to pardon him. Nevertheless, pardon is a demand of love. When two persons love each
other, if an offense to love has been committed, only a pardon
given permits love to survive. If it is given, it must be within the
right conditions. To ask for pardon is costly: One makes himself
dependent upon the pardon that may be given to him, but which
also may be refused: Men are often hard on each other. God is
rich in mercy, and He always forgives when a person demands it
of Him sincerely and in truth.

Pardon structures the life of love. It belongs to the breathing of love. There is no love without pardon, for if there were,
that would mean that when one loves, one becomes perfect! But
no! One improves himself, but he never attains this state where
he would be exempt from having to be excused or pardoned of
an offense. Thus, pardon must be practiced. We mustn't over-
dramatize the common life and say that there necessarily must

be moments of grave conflict in every human communion. Not all couples are divided or separated, and not all of them tear themselves apart! But that does happen. There is also pardon of small offenses and then a habitual practice of pardon, a state of spirit disposed to pardon that must be simple. We recall the kiss that parents and children exchange in the evening before going to bed.

Reconciliation washes away small offenses, but it also protects from great offenses. Pardon confers a *habitus* of communion, so desired that one gives it the means for this pardon. For the baptized, this assumes a vital bond with God's pardon. I ask myself how it is possible to live out pardon within a family when none of its members drink of the pardon of God in the Sacrament of Reconciliation. Pardon is not there in order to dramatize, or to place extra weight upon the members of the family. Pardon is the fruit of an interior demand. When you feel that you have wounded someone else, then you necessarily feel the need at your core to be reconciled with that person. When one person says to another, "I forgive you," it is as if he says to him: "I again make a covenant with you." And you imagine how fitting this practice is to the relationship between spouses! That is to say, "I give all of my love to you again, and all of the rights that you have upon me, I offer them to you anew" . . . exactly as in the parable of the Prodigal Son. The son returns to his father and stammers excuses. His father does not even allow him to express himself but instead embraces him and covers him with kisses. This is not a distant handshake! He gives back to the son all of the rights to his goods, along with a ring and sandals and a beautiful tunic, and he celebrates his son's return with a banquet.

I am thinking of two brother archbishops who were nuncios on the Arabian Peninsula and in North Africa, in Iran, and in the Maghreb. For them, the great difference—the fundamental difference—between Islam and Christianity is that in Christianity there is pardon.

J.L. I think so as well. Christ has taught us pardon.

For the family, could you tackle the question of pardon in the case of "conjugal" infidelity? In thought, in act. Does the demand of love not go further than simple acts?

J.L. Among all of the wounds that can affect conjugal communion, the wound caused by infidelity is of grave importance. Infidelity wounds profoundly because it reaches what is the very essence of the covenant. The conjugal covenant is exclusive, total, and without reservation by its nature. Infidelity is a betrayal of the covenant, a wound that is very deep. Moreover, it is so profound that in numerous pieces of legislation, the act of adultery founds the right of the betrayed partner to demand the dissolution of marriage at the civil level. This was still the case in France several years ago.

At the religious level, things cannot be presented in these terms. One cannot deny the gravity of the infidelity of adultery. Within Christian marriage, added to the human betrayal is the reality of a wound inflicted upon the sacrament of marriage, a kind of profanation, even if the persons who commit adultery don't think about wanting to profane the sacrament. In fact, there is something holy and sacred in marriage that no longer is accounted for in the case of adultery. It is a grave act committed against the husband or wife, and against God. It is also committed against the children; they are children of a conjugal communion, of a father and mother who are united within this irrevocable covenant of marriage. Adultery creates a new situation, in which the covenant of the spouses loses something of its consistency and its contents.

Looking at the facts, pastors of souls and of those who accompany couples know that adultery is one of the two or three faults that are the most difficult to pardon. When love has been betrayed, it is very difficult to pardon for a reason that is anthropological in character: The betrayal of love takes away the conditions within which love must be able to express trust in the future. It ruins or weakens the capacity to trust in him or her who has betrayed us. At the level of communion of the spouses, the covenant is profoundly wounded.

However, when spouses truly united in the sacrament of marriage sincerely desire that their covenant last and renew itself, conjugal communion responds. In the face of a grave ordeal such as betrayal or adultery, the reaction must be proportionate. The covenant must be renewed, something that can be done only through a pardon—one that is not superficial but rather is serious, deep, and reflected upon, for the baptized must drink of the sacramental source of reconciliation. To the degree to which there is a serious sin that one desires to pardon, sacramental pardon—which habitually should nourish the spirituality of the spouses—gives the opportunity to the one who was betrayed to drink of the power of Christ's pardon. Christ is by definition He whose love was betrayed. God is He whose love always is betrayed by sin and the faults of men. However, He makes a covenant again with men by pardoning them. What is possible for God is not immediately possible for man; however, it can become so through the grace and strength of God, through sacramental strength received in prayer. This case requires a journey of profound truth. Pardon can only be given in the right conditions, and thus he who has betrayed must come back to himself, form a new heart and purify it, making it available once again exclusively for love of the other. He must reconcile himself with his spouse and also with God. It is a difficult thing that requires time. Obviously, not all betrayals have the same effect: There are exponentially greater betrayals, such as extraconjugal liaisons that last for a long time. When betrayal has spread across several years, and conjugal and family life has enjoyed all appearances of a true communion, pardon is very difficult: It will encounter very particular obstacles for forgiveness to unfold and bear fruit. It will demand on the part of the betrayed spouse a sometimes heroic effort. A spouse who has decided to pardon, understanding this fault, and who says to his or her spouse, "I again make a covenant with you," accomplishes a Christian act at a very high level and with great dignity. The Christian is ready to go as far as pardoning his enemies. He who has betrayed love has acted in some manner as an enemy. This causes further suffering, because it is this love that has been betrayed at the symbolic, human, spiritual, and ethical levels.

In the pardon of Christ—who forgives everyone who has betrayed His infinite love—only one way forward is possible, one that is strict and very demanding, and orients toward pardon. When the wound of adultery cannot heal, in particular when the spouse who has betrayed is not ready to stop the betrayal, one knows that victims react differently according to their personal temperaments and histories. Some people pardon even then, leaning upon the pardon of Christ, which is always being given again, tirelessly, even though we do not stop betraying Him. On the other hand, others cannot find in themselves the possibility of expressing love.

Generally, it is good not to expect irreversible situations. Couples experiencing difficulty need the accompaniment of a priest and the presence of solid friends. One can counsel them to make a retreat or a pilgrimage together, or a trip with just the two of them, in order to re-create the covenant with strong symbolic gestures. Pardon can take time, but once it is given, it must not be taken back. He who asks for pardon sincerely places himself in dependence upon the one whom he has wounded, and he does it with the hope of being pardoned. He must leave this situation that he has caused through his acts and choices. He waits for pardon to be given to him; one cannot say anything *a priori* about the forms of pardon, which vary a lot according to the situations and personal histories.

Conjugal infidelity is thus very grave, for it touches upon the very essence of conjugal communion. Infidelity often is the end of a process that does not begin with the unfaithful act. The imagination is often crammed with images and symbolic messages having an erotic connotation. It is very difficult to avoid suggestions without particular vigilance. Today people are bombarded by millions of images. This issue is of particular concern in the case of young people, who have little protection. The imagination must be purified constantly.

There is a pollution of the imagination.

J.L. Yes, it profoundly affects the psychological conditions of communion. The man who is not vigilant in prayer becomes vulnerable to this type of suggestion. As for the consent one gives to these thoughts and this kind of imagination, this must be combated at its root and be handed over ceaselessly to the mercy of God. These are faults that one must have the simplicity and humility to confess to God because, in addition to the pardon of faults, the sacrament also gives the grace to be able to resist them in the best conditions in the future. The spouses receive the means of grace that permit them to be faithful even in the intimacy of thoughts.

Are there privileged means for fighting against these images?

J.L. Yes, spiritual means accompanied by prudence. The practice of adoration of the exposed Blessed Sacrament purifies the imagination considerably. It is the purity of God in the Sacrament of the Altar.

One always has difficulty controlling our imaginary follies that run wild.

J.L. Yes, and I believe that God has the capacity to heal even the depths of the imagination. This is part of the greatness of God and of His love. He heals us even within the most profound level of our soul and comes to help us in our every vulnerability.

We leave the question of pardon now in order to return to a more contextual question. Authority today has become an anachronistic notion in the bosom of the family and in educational institutions. Among believers, the positions taken by the Magisterium of the Church are more and more misunderstood as an unwarranted intrusion into private life. How might we be faithful to the Tradition and to the teachings of the Church while remaining in today's world without marginalizing ourselves?

J.L. The question touches the way we see the Tradition. The Church refers to that which has been transmitted to her by Christ, and which she has transmitted through the Apostles and their successors. We are speaking of a living deposit that never ceases to be enriched and further clarified. Concerning matters of faith, the proclamation of a new dogma is very rare. This occurs because of the necessity that truths known and already present in the faith of the entire Church be clarified

or elaborated at a conceptual level. I think of Pius XII's definition of the dogma of the Assumption in 1950. The way we
see the Tradition is decisive. When we consider the Tradition
of the Church from the first centuries, the various theological
developments, the deepening of doctrinal understanding in the
Middle Ages, and the dogmatic contributions of the Council
of Trent and Vatican Councils I and II, we are struck by a richness that is new each time and integrates the entirety of what
has been brought forth previously. The Tradition transmits itself
and never ceases to be what it is; at the same time it is living,
spreads, blossoms, and grows.

What is the content of the Tradition? We have already spoken of the truths of faith and of dogmas. There are also truths
that concern human conduct in terms of what grounds it in the
eternal Law and that which expresses the latter, natural law. This
includes the precepts of the Decalogue as well as the teachings
of Christ in the Gospel. The teaching of Christ does not render
the Decalogue obsolete. It exceeds it while assuming it. Christ
does not abolish the Law but fulfills it. When the Church makes
a pronouncement today on moral matters, she simply exercises
the charism that is hers as Teacher of truth, because of the gift
that has been given to her: the indestructible assistance of the
Holy Spirit guaranteed by Christ to His Church, to Peter and
the Apostles, and to the successors of the Apostles. The Church
leans on this certitude. Inasmuch as she is the Church, she does
not doubt. Thus, there exists a moral deposit of the Church's
teaching, tied to the teachings of Revelation, upon which the
Church herself has spoken. In *Humanae Vitae*, Paul VI refers to
the natural law. The reason for this is that the Church has the
competency to interpret the natural law and fundamental goods:
In this way, the good of human life implies the question of the
conservation, protection, and unconditional defense of life from

150   JEAN LAFFITTE
conception until its natural end. This explains the positions of the Church in these areas. She categorically rejects abortion. In this, she repeats what the *Didaché* said at the beginning of the second century: Between the Christians and the pagans, there is no apparent difference. They eat, they dress themselves, they do not distinguish themselves by anything special, except by that which they refrain from doing: In particular, the Christian does not kill an infant in its mother's womb. I insist upon the fact that the natural law is not an arbitrary disciplinary norm, which imposes a limitation upon people that it could just as well not impose. Norms of discipline also exist within the Church; she also has a law, for she constitutes a society. These disciplinary norms are the expression of a spiritual good that the Church intends to protect and promote. In order to conclude on this point, it seems to me that to be faithful to the teachings of the Church gives rise to contradictions; however, this does not marginalize the faithful. On the contrary, it gives us the means to situate ourselves better in the world.

Would the family also have a role to play in the regeneration of the ecclesial institution? How do you envisage this? Do you have concrete examples to give us?

J.L. The family, by what she lives out at the natural and spiritual levels as a communion between different members, founded upon the quest for a common good, teaches all of the Church that all believers are called to live these values of Christian communion. This applies to each person, those who are not committed to a conjugal and family relation as well as those who are consecrated in celibacy for the Kingdom. As the "domestic church," the family clearly teaches that all religious community truly must be a praying communion. In many congregations, the members meet to pray several times per day, which grounds and develops the fraternal spirit. The family is paradigmatic in this way. If a community of religious brothers or sisters does not establish a relationship between its members of the same fraternal quality as that which exists between brothers and sisters of a family that get along, this could create a spiritual family that does not live out fraternal charity. It is the straw that breaks the camel's back! What is the meaning of a group of consecrated people who do not live in fraternal love? How is it useful to the Kingdom? It is a juxtaposition of persons who run along all alone. But if you run along all alone in the Church, who will show you the demands of charity? There is no sanctification within the Church that does not take place through charity and love of neighbor. There are no saints strong on spiritual matters who would be exempt from the simple service of loving brothers, or from this position of servant we mentioned at the beginning, from attention to others, from the duties of human and Christian solidarity, from helping those in need, from active compassion extended to others. The bonds of love in the bosom of the loving family teach simplicity in relationship and service.

Do you see a connection between the crisis of authority and the current failure of the political class? How could the family generate new life for the city?

J.L. It is very difficult to speak of the political class as a homogenous whole. The political class includes a great number of people who have different responsibilities at many diverse levels. It is certain that the more the level of political responsibility increases, the more there is a generalization of competencies and tasks that render the exercise of that responsibility more complex and delicate. There is the risk of watering down the relation between the political official and the citizen. Among a large number of politicians, there is a certain sense of personal responsibility, and I sincerely think this. Nevertheless, certain democratic mechanisms sometimes make it impossible for a politician to communicate the best of himself and to allow a fruitful action to unfold over a long period of time. I refer in particular to electoral cycles that are close at hand and to the necessity of convincing at any price, since the majority will determine adherence or lack of adherence to certain politics. This is often detrimental to content and to its further development. In certain domains, there is no clear perspective in taking decisions into account. A typical case in my opinion is that of politics of the family and demographic questions. No politician will get involved in a program that will bear fruit in twenty-five years. There are important problems of which one speaks at congresses or universities but which do not lead to the courageous political decisions that would impose renunciations on citizens and leaders.

Today, there is a kind of precariousness in politics. The politician seems to live from election to election. What mobilizes his energies is survival. How does he tackle the next election? How does he present such a point to the citizens so as not to alarm them, discourage them, or irritate them? How does he convince the lobbies? How does he articulate the game of alliances? How does he orient himself vis-à-vis international organizations? How does he deal with the media? At all levels, there are very delicate relational and social balances within a system of consultative machinery and increasingly sophisticated decisions. I personally already have heard politicians express doubt out loud in relation to the influence they were able to have on the course of things, in particular in grave areas. The exercise of politics today does not integrate into its historical memory the arguments it advances to get laws voted. When a law is voted upon based on certain arguments, ten or twelve years later one has completely forgotten what motivated the voting-in of that law. We know this well in the regulation of areas touching upon the respect for life (abortion and euthanasia). Certain lobbies have understood perfectly how to promote reforms through successive advances.

Here we have a balanced response. One would love for politicians to have such a spirit present among them!

J.L. I have respect for men who manifest a sincere concern for the common good. No person can carry the moral weight of society by himself. In the politician's charter, one should insist upon the fact that no person should ever vote in favor of a law that is against his conscience. The discipline of political parties should take this point into consideration. Party votes concerning social problems seem to me truly to limit the freedom of politicians.

Finally, within this perspective, should the Church not seek to form elites more?

J.L. The response is yes. She does so in certain countries, but here in Europe she has done so badly, since public education has wanted to distance itself categorically from its historical patrimony and to banish everything near and far that brings to mind the Church's teaching.

This question is asked in different terms from one continent to another. In Western Europe and particularly in France, we belong to an unwritten tradition that wants politicians to abstain from stating their faith and to maintain the object of their belief or nonbelief strictly within the private sector. We often justify this by theorizing the need to keep civil and confessional approaches separate, but it is not the case everywhere. It is a tradition, moreover, that one has the right to subject things to critical examination.

When citizens give their adherence through their vote to a politician or to a political party, it would not be at all useless for them to know the philosophical or religious point of view of the politician they propose to accept as an official responsible for the common good. It is not at all indifferent to know whether or not a politician comes from a predominantly rationalistic tradition or is Christian, agnostic, or anticlerical. It is not at all indifferent to him who chooses to know if, on an issue he sees as vitally important, he can expect a certain position out of such and such a politician.

Right now, grave social problems are being debated in the area of bioethics: the choice of a family model, education, how interpersonal relations are conceived, women's rights, and a host of important questions concerning persons. It would not be at all superfluous if someone were better able to know a man or woman to whom he eventually will give his support. The path of strict separation is typically French. Very often you hear politicians saying: I am a believer, but I put my faith in parentheses when I am in public debate. I do not have to take my faith into account when I make a political decision. Underlying this is an idea that the Christian faith, the faith of the Church, within a tradition where the Catholic Church is present, is only one opinion among others.

You understand that the Christian who thinks and affirms this does not really believe in the legitimacy of his own faith, since he does not attribute to it the power to inspire his political action. On the other hand, there are different traditions in other countries: politicians affirm whether they are Christians or not. People vote first based on a candidate's abilities and competencies, but they want to know what inspires their positions taken in one or another sense. This is the case in the United States and among Anglo-Saxon countries, but also in several countries of Latin America and Asia. The idea of belonging to a religious tradition is not taboo.

Obviously, it's good to guard against any manipulation of the faith, but it would be a great loss to exclude a dimension of capital importance from one's reflection on the common good, inasmuch as religious action also has an important social dimension. The essence of a religious tradition is to care about God, but also for men and their good. And the essence of a political action is also to care for the common good of men.

The faithful God is patient: If God narrows their path, it is in order to lead them with more tenderness and concern: "With the Lord one day is as a thousand years, and a thousand years as one day. The Lord is not slow about His promise as some count slowness, but is forbearing toward you, not wishing that any should perish, but that all should reach repentance" (2 Pet. 3:8–9). Could you conclude this chapter on authority by presenting to us the link that unites authority and obedience within love, and thus freedom with time?

J.L. We have to begin, I think, with a reflection on time. Everything we have been talking about is situated in time. Time is the object of a human perception that consists of seeing things in their succession. This is proper to man. He has an intelligence and above all a self-awareness that is structured according to the great divisions of time: the past, the future, and the present. There is a difference in philosophical status between the past and the present, and between the future and the present.

The present is the only space of time within which man is able to act. The future does not belong to him, even if he is able to anticipate certain elements. As for the past, it is no longer there; one no longer can act upon it. One can act on the memory of the past in order to distort it, but he cannot act upon past time in the sense that we have indicated.

In addition, when you want to connect time with the question of freedom, as you do in your question, we must take within time the only part that can be in relation to human freedom: the present. Of course, the future also comes into play indirectly, by the fact that the decisions and actions taken now will doubtless have repercussions for the future. On the other hand, the status of human freedom cannot be appreciated except by considering the present moment. It is within the present that a person's freedom is exercised. This is a very important point.

But if man gains a certain perception of time, he cannot comprehend in the same thought what time could be for God. Time does not exist for God, inasmuch as God is eternal: He embraces the totality of time. He did not begin to exist, and He will never stop existing. There is thus the totality of everything that appears to us as time, which for God is a single "instant." To say this is to speak a metaphysical truth, but not to understand it! We cannot have a sensible perception of the time lived by God, if I may put it this way, because we do not see what "lived by God" means. What we know is that God is present at every moment of history, which He embraces in all of His power. God is not dependent on a succession of moments, as is the case for the creatures that we are. On the other hand, since God has created creatures, He knows their inner workings. He also knows what the succession of time is for the man He has created. The action of God necessarily makes itself known to man in a progressive fashion and enters within the succession of time. What appears to us as a delay is tied to a pedagogical intention of God. Thus, we cannot have in one instant the totality of the logic of the actions or nonactions of God, of all that in Him appears to us to be action or passivity. That does not at all render useless or illegitimate the sometimes lively questioning that we can have toward God. Such questioning manifests a supplication, a prayer, a request for understanding that is superior to time.

When the Christian prays and requests the light of the Spirit of God, he enters into a different, more penetrating but also more calm, understanding of what can be a series of past events. He is able to see a kind of harmony, a Providential coherence, in the sequence of different episodes that he has been able to traverse in his existence. In this way, he can have more and more trust in God, who is the true master of history. He is the conqueror, and His victory is present in spite of the evil that exists in the world. These are not speculations. Rather, it is what we know of God and what has been revealed to us within the mysteries of His divine life that the Holy Spirit communicates to us.

We are able to elicit a small idea of this by meditating upon certain acts that we accomplish, which would lose all of their meaning if what we have just said were false. These are acts of a liturgical nature. These acts are not only acts of memory, but also acts that make present that which has happened. In celebrating the Eucharist, you celebrate an event that you remember, and you proclaim its present power and fruitfulness for the future: the expectation of eternal life. "We proclaim Your Death, O Lord, and profess Your Resurrection until You come again": It must be understood that we are proclaiming His Resurrection now. We become contemporaries of the Resurrection that happened two thousand years ago. There is a sort of abolition of time that, in the liturgical act, makes us contemporaries of the episodes that God has permitted us to live with Him. We adhere to this in faith. Faith permits us to adhere to the presence of God, to God who is present.

It is thus that time and freedom can be articulated for a Christian. He is conscious of the limits of his nature that sees only a succession of moments. However, his faith permits him to have the intuition that in God there is an instant that embraces the totality of time, which escapes us, but that this instant spans all of man's history. He makes Himself known through the history of His chosen people, through the mysteries of the Incarnation and Redemption, through the gift of the Holy Spirit and the fruits of the Spirit to which He gives rise within His Church. We can only perceive all of this in succession, but in the liturgical act we are made contemporaries of a historical event that truly took place: The Passion and Resurrection of Christ are made present to us. Man discovers the mystery of time that can unite us to God's eternity, for he sees that eternity transcends time and provides its ultimate meaning.

SIX

The School of Love
and the Chain of the Living

For the Lord is good, His steadfast love endures forever, and
His faithfulness to all generations.

(PS. 100:5)

The Lord, a God merciful and gracious, slow to anger, and
abounding in steadfast love and faithfulness.

(EXOD. 34:6)

Pierre and Véronique Sanchez: *Our society tends at times
toward rupture and fragmentation. The proportion of persons who
live alone continues to escalate. Christian love, for which the family
wants to be a hearth, is also proposed fully to single persons. What
does the Church have to say to single people?*

Bishop Jean Laffitte: We find here the question of vocation.
I believe that the question of single people in part comes from
the difficulty of thinking of the single person who has not chosen to be so, while one has brought to light the two modalities
of response to God's calling to love: marriage and consecrated
virginity. And so, to be a single person . . . Would it not be a

state of life? My way of tackling this question is the following.
Too often, one sees the question of a state of life as a personal
choice. In a state of life, one examines what the choice is and
also the response to a calling. God calls by way of numerous me-
diations. In conjugal love, a man comes to encounter a woman
and sees that she will be his companion for all of his life. This
is a mediation through which God can call to conjugal love; it
involves a concrete experience. The same thing applies for the
vocation to consecrated celibate life. This vision, too exclusively
centered upon the person's choice instead of insisting upon the
choice that God makes, renders unintelligible the single state
that is undergone and suffered. For the single person can say to
himself: "I never had the luck to meet a young woman whom I
could think would become my wife for all of my life. And until
I receive further inspiration from the Lord, I cannot say He has
made me see that He is calling me to the religious or consecrated life or to the priesthood." A person who is not married
and who is not consecrated does not stop being called any further to sanctity. There is a sanctity that can unfold in a manner
different than through the visible gift made to the Church by a
consecrated person or perhaps in the formation of a family.

   I myself do not think that the single state is *a priori* a failed
life, either at the spiritual level or at the psychological. This is
my conviction. However, the single life undergone, and thus to
say not selected, can effectively stop essential questions from
being asked: The years pass, and one never asks the question
of the meaning of giving one's own life. On the other hand, if
one asks this question, he then can see that a single life can be
a life given under other forms, under other modalities. You have
people who choose to remain single because of a mission that
they deem important to fulfill. Even in the secular life, certain
people desire to consecrate their life to their art, to a mission, to

research. No single person is deprived *a priori* of love under all of the forms that do not belong specifically to religious consecration or to conjugal love. The gift of self, service, active compassion, social engagements, clubs and societies, and indeed other activities offer a great number of opportunities to give oneself. Services that are so demanding that they exclude conjugal life also exist.

A single life not chosen should be thought of as an expression of the free choice of God, who can call someone to get married or to be consecrated in celibacy, and who also may not formulate a particular call. All the same, the call to sanctity and to love holds for each person, above all for the baptized. One must reflect upon this in order to help persons who suffer. In effect, there is within single life a difficult dimension of affective solitude. It is uncomfortable to face the difficulties of life alone. Nobody is set aside from divine election.

Could we now address the case of divorced persons? The Church teaches us that situations must be distinguished:

> Pastors must know that, for the sake of truth, they are obliged to exercise careful discernment of situations. There is in fact a difference between those who have sincerely tried to save their first marriage and have been unjustly abandoned, and those who through their own grave fault have destroyed a canonically valid marriage. Finally, there are those who have entered into a second union for the sake of the children's upbringing . . .
> I earnestly call upon pastors and the whole community of the faithful to help the divorced, and with solicitous care to make sure that they do not consider themselves as separated from the Church, for as baptized persons they can, and indeed must, share in her life (Familiaris Consortio 84).

J.L. The question of divorced persons who have remarried is a question that has been hotly debated in the Church for about twenty years. This question gives rise to a great number of publications, many of which clamor for a change in the Church's discipline in what concerns access to Eucharistic communion. One often forgets that the Church is not first of all taking a kind of disciplinary measure. She simply acts from the reality of what sacramental marriage is: a covenant of the spouses, with the presence of Christ who comes to make a covenant with the spouses. The Eucharist, too, is a covenant of Christ with the baptized, and in particular with the spouses who receive Communion. There is a real, deep spiritual and theological relationship between the sacrament of the Eucharist and the sacrament of matrimony, as we already have had the occasion to say.

At the theological level, the question that one asks is this: "Does the Church have the possibility to allow all of the people committed to second, third, or fourth unions to receive Eucharistic Communion and, at the same time, to say that marriage is indissoluble, and that its natural indissolubility is reinforced by the fact that Christ is a stakeholder in this covenant? How do we divide Christ?" That is the question. How do we say that Christ maintains the value and validity of a first union from which He does not uncommit—if it is valid, and I specify this point for it is not always the case—and at the same time how can this same Christ be received within a Eucharistic covenant with integrity? The question is not first of all a moral one but rather is a matter of taking into account the very nature of the Eucharist, what it is, and what Eucharistic Communion implies.

However, there is a feeling of injustice felt by divorced people who have remarried. During the course of the Sunday assembly, remarried divorced persons are the only people who don't Communicate. All of the other faithful receive Communion, whatever the spiritual state of their soul may be. When I told you that this question has been asked very pointedly over the past twenty years, I wanted to say that this question existed before, but nobody made it a theological, moral, or spiritual problem. It was understood that if you had not been able to live in solitude after a divorce and were remarried civilly, you did not access Eucharistic Communion. However, you were not the only one who didn't receive! A few decades ago, the faithful who participated in the Eucharist would only approach Eucharistic Communion when they thought they were in the spiritual state to do so. A remarried divorced person of the time found himself among those people who did not Communicate. Today, they are the only ones! There's the injustice! This problem does not come from the discipline of the Church, understood rightly. Such injustice arises from the fact that so great a number of baptized persons think it doesn't matter if they go to receive the Body of Christ in a spiritual state that would without a doubt require sacramental purification. You have people who have not gone to confession for one year, for two years or more, and who go to receive Communion! The injustice resides in the lack of respect, of love, and of veneration toward the sacrament of the Eucharist. A remarried divorced person who suffers profoundly from not accessing Communion shows much more love toward the Body of Christ than those people used to casual Communion.

Interestingly, moreover, I would like to remark that it was at the moment when generalized access to Eucharistic Communion developed that the worship of the Most Blessed Sacrament stopped being witnessed publicly, as the practice of Eucharistic adoration was suppressed for many years. Adoration is the place where one becomes conscious of his personal unworthiness! I know people who have told me they abstained from Communicating after having spent a long while in front of the Blessed

Sacrament, because they had discovered the need for sacramental pardon. I have witnessed this several times myself as a priest. The less you venerate the majesty of God within the simplicity of the Sacrament of the Altar, the more you consider it completely normal to go to Communion without preparing yourself. Yet when we Communicate, it is really Christ whom we receive.

Allow me to go even further. I have seen paths toward sanctity on the part of remarried divorced persons who, even without understanding the Church's discipline at the beginning, strove to practice it. While abstaining from going to Communion, they continued to participate regularly in the Eucharist, to pray together, to commit themselves within the services of the Church. They acquired a refined sensitivity and respect for the Eucharist such that they were traveling a true path of sanctification. What I say here may seem demanding, but apart from all polemics, let us recognize that the suffering of remarried divorced persons should make us reflect upon the manner in which we ourselves habitually approach the Holy Table.

The Synod for the Family of 1980 that gave rise to the postsynodal exhortation *Familiaris Consortio* developed at length the distinction between Eucharistic Communion and spiritual communion. Remarried divorced persons are fully invited through spiritual communion to participate in the sacrifice of Christ celebrated in the Eucharist, as in all of the mysteries of the Christian life. Eucharistic Communion with the Body and Blood of Christ makes explicit, translates, and expresses this spiritual communion; that is to say, the adherence of the faithful to the mystery of the Redemption celebrated during the Mass. People have often confused spiritual communion and Eucharistic Communion, thinking mistakenly that someone who had not had the opportunity to go to Communion was outside of the Church, outside of the communion of the Church. Such an interpretation is unfounded. There is no access to Eucharistic Communion during the time that a situation of incompatibility lasts in an objective way; but that is not to say there is an absence of spiritual communion concerning the mystery, or a lack of true belonging to the Church.

There is in effect a focus upon the non-access to Communion without taking into account other aspects and riches of the Christian life.

J.L. Inasmuch as remarried divorced persons do not have access to the Eucharist, they have the feeling of being excluded. In the vast number of cases, however, a first union went badly. At times, there is doubt concerning the validity of the sacrament of marriage; however, one lacks the elements that could prove a possible invalidity. A great number of elements enter into the situation of persons who have contracted a second marriage. One does not think enough about everything that causes suffering to persons in these particular situations. Those who have made the interior journey of accepting not to Communicate give a true testimony of love for the Church, which even leads certain persons among them to commit within spiritual families or associations to helping those who find themselves in the same situation.

In your approach, you have counseled remarried divorced persons?

J.L. Yes, on several occasions. I have also had the opportunity to accompany remarried divorced persons. I sometimes have seen extraordinary cases. I remember one couple in particular: They had Communicated for years because a priest had encouraged them in a superficial fashion to do so. After some time, they noticed that the fact of Communicating was not giving them the joy for which they had hoped. They then asked themselves the question why, and understood that they had never made the spiritual journey to enter into what the Church asked of them, despite some of the advice that had been given to them. Common prayer pushed them to make the decision to live as brother and sister. This was a way of returning to Communion. It must be said that these persons were engaged in an adult ecclesial movement, prayed, and went to Mass every Sunday. There are a certain number of similar cases that we don't hear much about.

When we were young, in fact, many of the faithful stayed seated during Communion.

J.L. Yes. If someone had not confessed for a long time, he abstained from going to Communion, and no one found fault in this form of the Church's sacramental praxis!

We have all been generated. With our children, we again live out the education that we received from our parents, including within the domain of the faith transmitted within the family, by the family. We quote Karol Wojtyła:

We have become for them a threshold which they
    cannot cross without effort,
to reach their new homes—the homes of their own
    souls.

It is well, at least, if they do not stumble—
We live in them for a very long time.
When they grow up under our eyes, they seem to
    become inaccessible,
like impermeable soil, but they have already
    absorbed us.
And though outwardly they shut themselves off,
inwardly we remain in them
and—a frightful thought—their lives somehow test
our own creation, our own suffering
(how else can one talk of love in the past tense?).[23]

J.L. In a profound and poetic fashion, this passage from *The Jeweler's Shop* shows that there is no education without suffering. The price of transmission and of fruitfulness is the suffering of the one who loves. This is true for parents and for educators alike. The more a child grows, the more his freedom seems to lead him into journeys that are totally distant and autonomous, where he will not make reference to his parents. You know that a seed has been planted, but you will not necessarily see the seed sprout. This question makes us think a little sadly of the transmission of the faith. The suffering of parents who have transmitted the Christian faith to children who then distance themselves, and sometimes have even fought to the point of making some absurd choices in life, is a suffering that is very widespread. These parents live out a particular trial where they no longer perceive that they have sown anything. Within this configuration, the text of *The Jeweler's Shop* enjoys a strong existential consistency that makes it a profoundly moving text.

---

23 Karol Wojtyła, *The Jeweler's Shop*, trans. B. Taborski. Ignatius Press, 1992, pp. 78–79.

But often our children lead us far, very far toward life. What parent will not acknowledge the fact that his or her children have, in some way, brought his or her own education to completion? Could you speak to us about the education of parents by their children, including in the question of conjugal life?

J.L. When children grow up and acquire their autonomy, they will take up their existence in a manner that will have some characteristics in common with what they experienced at home, but others which will distinguish them as well in numerous respects. In this area, children will not necessarily distance themselves from a perfectly successful model, or do less well, for the reverse can happen. They can realize something that the parents have not realized. To educate means to give to a child or to an adolescent the means for his freedom and his future autonomy. Moreover, this is not limited to the familial sphere but applies to the teaching of the schoolteacher, the professional, and the spiritual director. When the children become autonomous, the parents rejoice even if they sometimes feel a bit useless. Additionally, children become autonomous when the parents stop their professional activity. There is a kind of separation, like a detachment that parents must have in relationship to what they have done and taught. The child in his own way brings to fruition the gifts that he has received; this begins through the choice of career and profession that does not correspond necessarily to what the parents have dreamt. The gift of an education does not have to return to its source in the form of a copy conforming to what the parents were able to do. When the parents have understood and accepted this, they learn much from their child and enter into a new relationship with him.

And we go both toward the future and toward the past. We let ourselves be guided, for example, by the tutelary presence of a grandfather who died before we could share with him everything that we had in our heart. The status reserved to the elderly in our societies is a silent scandal. How do we unite family and the welcoming of aged persons who are more and more numerous, and more and more marginalized?

J.L. The presence of the elderly in families has become a problem only recently. Until only a short while ago, all families had one or two aged persons with them. They did not live necessarily in the house of their children or of their grandchildren, but they often came staying for several weeks. A natural familiarity existed between generations, between grandparents and grandchildren. If today the proportion of aged persons becomes greater and greater, it is not due only to extending life expectancy, but also because of the disproportionate lack of young persons who should have existed. The balance becomes an imbalance, and this is a novelty. In demography, one calls this very simply "the aging of the population." European countries are, along with Japan, those where aging is the most considerable. The family is reduced there to the simplest expression, to one child at most. One no longer puts up with the presence of an aged person. Confined and marginalized beyond the living framework of a family, the elderly seem to form a population set apart. Moreover, the economy, tourism, the markets, and finance have taken note of this reality: One speaks of a third age, and now of a fourth age, with preferential allowances and particular services, as if the elderly formed a homogenous group. What is homogenous in this crisis is their neglect and distancing from the family, families that they founded! We must observe that this is a phenomenon endemic to our culture, and, by the grace of God, does not exist in other cultures of the world.

Note that this tendency to classify persons within categories of age is spreading. One speaks of young people, of adults, and of the elderly. The relegation of young people to a separate, well-compartmentalized category accentuates the gap between generations. You may remember the recent drought in France, and the death of numerous aged persons that it provoked. We discovered on this occasion that the persons were strangers in the lives of their own families. This was a disgraceful episode for France, a humiliation for our country. This dramatic episode reveals the profound loneliness of the elderly and at the same time the incapacity of our society to remedy it.

To conclude, we know that the concept of experience is dear to you. It appears in the use of examples; the example is always the most effective teaching. I would hope for us to finish by speaking of holiness, mentioning some figures of holiness, for example couples who have lived their faith, their sacrament of marriage, and the welcoming of children and their education under God's gaze. Christians need models, saints who encourage them and who draw them upward. Do you have examples for families?

J.L. Holiness is fruitful and attractive. It is fruitful through the supernatural fruits of grace. But why is it attractive? True holiness cannot be sad. It is joyful and always demonstrates a profound harmony between saintly persons and the order of creation, the order of the world, and with God, the source of all that is created. A holy person carries in himself a certain number of virtues, values, charisms, and specific graces that are not abstractions but become incarnated values, living values, "expressions" of sanctity. Every saint has something to say to families.

We must realize that the Holy Spirit does not lack inventiveness in creating the grace of holiness in people. Holiness takes many different forms from one person to the next. It also happens that this holiness is hidden. It is not rare to see, in the person of a saint, the presence of a great apparent defect that seemingly renders the person less conformed to the criteria of media-friendly beauty or social success. How would we in our day put up with the holiness of Saint Benedict Labre, who traveled the roads of Europe and made his own every characteristic of the homeless today? However, the man was in constant dialogue with God, and he loved Him. The saints are surprising: The more they allow the strength of the Holy Spirit to enter them, the more they surprise us. A saint never bores, but he disturbs due to who he is. He is a living reproach for anyone who is living in lukewarmness. The saint is a paradoxical person in his manner of living, which is out of joint with worldly values. Some of the saints are greatly original, such as Saint Philip Neri.

There also is an ordinary holiness. At times, a person tells you: "Since I met you, it has been forty years that I have been praying for you each day!" You discover that the joys you have experienced during your life, the fruits that could be given, the errors that could have been avoided—all of this has something to do with the prayer of this humble person. There are persons in whom you were never interested and who were very significant in your life without your knowing it. When, through the grace of God, a little corner of the veil is lifted from the spiritual riches of these humble people, you catch a glimpse that there is a lesson of spiritual life, and their supernatural charity appears exemplary and truly attractive to you. A moment of grace is given to you that will bring you perhaps in your turn to pray for someone without his knowing, and you will offer a sacrifice for this person. Little by little, the solidarity proper to the communion of saints enters into your life, and in this manner exemplary holiness bears its fruits. Love communicates itself and spreads beyond itself. The example of love sparks in you the desire to love. One cannot shut it in; it communicates itself, expresses itself. Divine Providence from time to time offers us the opportunity to lift up a corner of the veil. When I was the director of pilgrimages at Paray-le-Monial, I had a collaborator close to me, one who died today, and I learned only after his death that he would get up every night for an hour in order to pray for the fruitfulness of the pilgrimage. What name would this carry if not that of sanctity? The person had entered along a pathway where the good of the Church, the rights of God, and the supernatural good of persons became a priority.

Of course, everything we have just said concerning sanctity applies, in a very specific way, to the couples to whom we have given our attention during our discussions. There is something very attractive in conjugal sanctity because it is a holiness that passes through the mediation of human love in its most brilliant and natural form. This is an extremely desirable sanctity.

Among the canonized saints, I think of Blessed Louis and Zélie Martin, the parents of Saint Thérèse. They did not live a life in common for very long, a little less than twenty years, because Zélie died relatively early. When you read their correspondence, you see the great delicacy of their love that unfolded and extended to all of their children.

What also do we say of the quality of love that united the philosophers Jacques and Raïssa Maritain, whom we already have mentioned. They are not canonized saints, but there is a very great, supernatural perfume in their love that transfigured their spousal life together. They enjoyed a very strong conjugal grace that was conscious, received, deepened, and expanded *ad extra*, since you know that the Maritains played a considerable role before the war in the conversion of dozens of persons within the literary and artistic milieus of Paris.

Luigi and Maria Beltrame Quattrocchi, still little known in France, were the first couple beatified by Pope John Paul II. Luigi was an Italian judge, very well known in the period between the two World Wars. The couple was exemplary in their Christian commitment, which each displayed in numerous milieus. The correspondence that they exchanged is edifying. All of the elements of a conjugal spirituality for our time are present. They are buried in the Roman Santuario della Madonna del Divino Amore. They saw successively their first three children become consecrated religious or priests. They lived this detachment as a kind of death to themselves and as a form of embracing solitude.

I would also like to mention a couple that died as martyrs, Cyprien and Daphrose Rugamba, who founded the Emmanuel Community in Rwanda and who were assassinated on April 7, 1994, at the beginning of conflicts there. This couple had ten children, and six of them were killed at the same time as they were, in their house. All of them were united in prayer to God. I had the grace to know them. In Rwanda, while interviewing those people who lived with them and who had known them well, I was able to understand that they had given the witness of a profoundly serene commitment to peace during their lives, refusing all escalation of ethnic rivalries and giving advice in this respect to numerous political officials. They paid for it with their lives.

All of these examples strengthen hope in us. Hope is a magnificent Christian virtue; it seems to me that one also can say that it is a familial virtue. When one gives his life, he makes an act of hope in the future. When someone educates, he educates in view of a future autonomy of his children, for whom he wishes true happiness. When one transmits education or instruction, he demonstrates hope. At the heart of the Christian couple and of the family, there is the mystery of hope: a natural, human hope and a supernatural hope when filled with God: Hope carries a family and its members toward the eternal future. Hope already makes the desired goods present. Each young person who is preparing to get married should transmit the conviction that there is a future for him, for his love, for his family, for his children, and for the society to whose common good he contributes. The family that grows together and is strengthened wagers that the society into which it is inserted is worthy of being served, and that consequently it is worth the trouble of working within it, of getting involved. Hope is a central virtue. We must ask it for ourselves, and wish it for those whom we love and desire to serve, along with all those who have accepted their vocation to love. Hope is at the heart of a culture of the family.